REDEMPTION SONGS

BY THE SAME AUTHOR

The Curve of the World: Into the Spiritual Heart of Yoga

REDEMPTION SONGS

A Year in the life
of a community prison choir

ANDY DOUGLAS

InnerWorld Publications
San Germán, Puerto Rico
www.innerworldpublications.com

Contents

LATE SUMMER

ONE

What Music Can Do

THE DIRECTOR LIFTS HER hands into the air in front of her and pauses. Within that pause lies all the energy of what's to come next. She dips her right hand, then, and brings us in on the downbeat.

A series of whole notes coalesce from our vocal cords—shimmering threads of sound—followed by quarter notes, a gathering cadence. We watch the director on her podium, her movements linked to our rhythmic expression as if tied to those shimmering threads. Quiet but intense, our voices blend, forming interlocking peaks of sound, until the clatter of food carts rumbling by in the hallway momentarily drowns out our harmonizing.

There are sixty of us in the choir this season, and we are spread out in three sprawling semicircles within the cinderblock rehearsal room, a range of men and women, young adults and the middle-aged, black, white, and Latino people, long hair and buzz cuts. Each of us stands in one of the four traditional sections: Tenor, Alto, Soprano or Bass.

Luke, a bass, is in the back row on the far side of the room. A short man with an angular face and a shock of black hair, he's singing wholeheartedly. But halfway through the song "Missing for So Long," he begins to twitch.

At first there's only a vague sense that something's up, the scraping of chair legs on tile floor, a fluttering of movement. People turn and look. Then there's a crash as Luke drops to his seat; he knocks the chair aside and falls to the floor.

The music goes on for one or two more measures, and then we trail off into silence. No one seems to know what to do. The activities coordinator springs into action, though; within seconds he's on his transponder, radioing for help. Not more than two minutes pass before a whole response team appears.

The medics make sure Luke's tongue is clear of his throat; a gurney is wheeled in and he's loaded on. The other choir members press back to give these people room to work. It's unsettling, but most of the insiders don't seem upset; they've seen this, and worse, before.

"He has these all the time," Everett, who's sitting next to me in the tenor section, says. "The medics got down here pretty quick, I'll say that for them, coming from all the way over on the far side of the prison." He tells me that Luke fell off a roof a few years ago, and landed on his head. Ever since, he's had these seizures.

Luke's body is still flailing a bit, but the six or so personnel form a phalanx around him to keep him still, and the gurney is wheeled out of the room, the officers moving like point men on security detail.

Everett doesn't say whether Luke was in prison when he fell, or if it happened before that. Or whether the accident somehow contributed to his being incarcerated. I can imagine a scenario where neurological damage led to a string of misfortunes—Luke having difficulty keeping a job and maintaining relationships, some bad decisions, his ultimately ending up in jail.

But maybe it was nothing like that. I can only speculate. One of the unwritten rules of this place is that people from the outside don't ask people on the inside what it was that landed them here. And they usually don't say.

Every Tuesday afternoon for six of the last eight years, I've driven or carpooled the nine miles from my home in Iowa City to the adjoining town of Coralville, where the Iowa Classification and Medical Center at Oakdale, a medium security men's prison, is located. To get there you pass a sea of townhouses lining the Interstate 80 corridor, and at the megamall exit turn north onto Highway 965. For several years, my girlfriend, Lois, also joined me, until she became busy with work.

The prison rises from amidst the sprawl of commercial development on the edge of town, a set of institutional buildings you might drive by without really noticing. Jockeying out of rush hour traffic and into the parking lot, I ease my car into a space near the main administration center. A gigantic American flag whips high in the breeze in front of the building, next to an Iowa flag and a Department of Corrections pennant. Bumper stickers on the cars of volunteers and prison staff offer mixed messages. "God Bless Everyone, No Exceptions"; "Out of Iraq Now." And, "Stop Global Whining."

I slide my driver's license across to the muscular Correctional Officer sitting behind the front desk. He flips through a box and pulls out my visitor's badge, which has my name and photo on it. Thanking him, I clip the badge to my shirt lapel, making sure it's firmly attached. Then I take a seat with the others, until it's time to line up and move quickly through the halls.

The volunteers gathered here are part of the Oakdale Community Choir (OCC), a performing chorale made up of 25 to 35 men serving time, and 25 to 30 community members, both men and women. For an hour and a half each week, we grapple with a range of choral music, mustering breath and will and vocal cords, preparing for two concerts at the end of each season—one for inmates in the prison, the other for the public (also held inside the prison).

The work is demanding, but it's also rewarding. As volunteers wade through the challenges of making music in this circumscribed environment, we gain glimpses into what life is like inside.

At the orientation before the beginning of my first season in the choir, a prison official walked our group of 15 new volunteers—choir members, a few AA facilitators, some religious instructors—through the basics.

"Remember, no open-toed sandals, sleeveless shirts, shorts, skirts above the knee, tight fitting clothing, or hooded sweatshirts are allowed inside the prison," he intoned. He made the protocol clear: passing through the corridors we were to walk close to the wall and pay attention to our surroundings.

"Potential danger," he warned, "lurks around every corner. Never let a prisoner walk behind you."

As if to put our understanding to the test, we were taken on a tour. Fluorescent lights flickered down the corridors, reflecting off shiny floors, and the scent of Pine-Sol lingered up to the next set of sliding doors. We shuffled past the cafeteria with its rows of institutional tables, past the cavernous gymnasium—waxed floor and dangling basketball hoops—and ended at the processing lockup, where prisoners are corralled when they first arrive.

Our group was mostly silent, drinking in the atmosphere. All along the route, men in T-shirts, blue jeans and white tennis shoes, and a few—if medical conditions warranted less restrictive clothing—in gray sweat pants, stared at us. Most wore their hair short, although a few had longer hair. Friendly curiosity flickered in some eyes, while other men's faces remained stony.

In the lockup, men peered at us from small rooms through tiny glass windows. They'd been in prison for only a day or so, or maybe only a few hours. I thought of the way mug shots tend to capture subjects in off-kilter, disheveled, unsmiling poses; these men seemed to be in a similar state of shock. A few stared without averting their gaze. What lay behind the guarded vulnerability of those eyes? Did these men recognize the pain they had caused others? Did they understand the pain they themselves were in? From this distance, there was no way of knowing.

Ushered away down the long halls toward the freedom of the front door, I couldn't help but wonder. What was it, apart from those inches of glass and concrete, that separated me from them?

On rehearsal day, the massive metal door into the main prison corridor slides open with a slow swoosh, choir volunteers file forward, the door clangs closed behind us and we're standing inside the first checkpoint, a decompression chamber for entering and leaving this high-pressure environment. I sidle up to some friends, Don and Kevin. They're talking baseball. Sliders and curve balls—do you know the difference?

"Sure," Kevin says, "a slider curves away in the opposite direction from a curveball. It's all in the way you hold the ball. Then there's the knuckleball. Sandy Koufax was famous for that."

Perhaps baseball, singing and incarceration all naturally dovetail as topics of conversation here, having in common as they do the importance of timing. But most of this small talk, I think, is meant to distract from the nerves that can accompany a penetration deeper into the heart of the prison, at least the first few times you come here.

After all, this is a space full of people who have committed serious crimes. If you were to buy into the narrative offered by some of the mass media, those living here were unfeeling, unthinking, dangerous people, men geared toward violence and opportunism. Why not put them away and forget about them?

Fairly quickly, I began to see that not all, or even most, of the people I met in prison were like that. And after several seasons in the choir, I feel more at ease each time we move single file out of the checkpoint and past the guardroom and the activity room/chapel where groups of prisoners are engaged in discussion.

Our column turns right, then right again.

We enter the "testing room," where on most days men take educational tests, perhaps trying for their GEDs. The cinderblock walls gleam white. Green ferns sprout near the windows, and computers hum in corners. A few not-particularly-motivating motivational posters adorn the walls: "Keep Trying!" "You Can Do It!"

The inside singers are already gathered in the room. Most of the guys who've signed up to sing are white, as are the majority of volunteers (this is Iowa, after all), but two or three African American men, and a couple of Latino men, have joined the group.

Prison authorities frown on physical contact, but many of us have come to skirt this restriction, shaking hands, even occasionally patting each other on the back. I say hello to an older white insider I'm friendly with, a stooped man with a grizzled beard.

"How's your health?"

"Still tickin'." He shrugs, his hands in his pockets.

"You've taken a licking and you're still tickin'?"

He smiles. "Yep."

Under "normal" circumstances, when you meet someone, there are a whole set of questions designed to facilitate the getting-to-know-you process. Where are you from? What do you do? What've you been up to these last ten years?

These questions are more or less out of bounds in prison. The outsiders don't ask about the crime that landed a person here, or about their sentence. And the insiders are definitely not supposed to ask where volunteers live, what they do, or anything about their personal lives. Sharing such information, we've been told, can be dangerous.

So, especially in the first few rehearsals of the season, we fumble for topics of conversation, engage in a little bantering between moments of rehearsing, reaching for a light mood, trying to puzzle out some meaning we can share, a peg to hang our mutuality on, the sweep of our lives rolling silently behind us.

I find a seat in the back row between Everett and Burt, two older white guys. Burt's white beard and hair mark him as one of the oldest members of the choir. His eyes twinkle, and he has a clear, strong and exceedingly high tenor voice. Everett is a large man with glasses, a paunch and an interesting backstory. As I said, I don't know a lot about most people in here, but about Everett, who likes to talk, I've learned a bit. For example, he grew up in Iran, son of a Texas oilman, and he speaks some Farsi.

The two are fond of each other. Burt says of Everett, "He grew up in Iran and Texas. So he didn't get much of an education."

To which Everett replies, "Yeah, I think you need to be a tenor. Ten—or twelve miles away from me." They laugh at each other's jokes, though they've heard them before.

We form a circle around the perimeter of the room. The director of the choir, Dr. Mary Cohen, steps onto the podium. Dark haired, nicely dressed, she's in her mid-forties. An associate professor of music at the University of Iowa, she brings a light touch to this work, cracking silly jokes, moving and gesturing big, drawing on a natural high-pitched energy.

She begins by leading us in the song "May You Walk in Beauty."

May you walk in beauty in a sacred way,
May you walk in beauty each and every day.
May the beauty of the fire lift your spirit higher.
May the beauty of the earth fill your heart with mirth.
May the beauty of the rain wash away your pain.
May the beauty of the sky teach your mind to fly.

The song comes out of a Native American tradition, and it's become a favorite here, a kind of anthem. People have created accompanying gestures, lifting their hands into the air at the word "higher" and clasping them over their chests at "fill your heart with mirth." As we watch each other across the arc of the circle, these movements seem to increase our feeling of community.

Burt, Everett and I, grooving on the tune, spontaneously lean our heads closer together, searching for tighter harmonies as if we were in a barbershop quartet. Burt shoots for the high notes, his pure tenor soaring above the rest of the choir, providing a canopy of sound. Everett takes the melody, and I aim for a mid-range harmony. Our voices intercept and then balance each other. *Teach your mind to fly.*

As we finish, the three of us, giddy with the effort of close harmony, glance at each other. Then we burst out laughing in delight at what music can do.

It started with the shaving of my facial hair and continued with the jumpsuit I was issued. I looked just like every other inmate. Even after I reached general population, the theme continued. All shoes were white. All pants are blue jeans. All shirts are blue and short sleeved. My coffee mug is just like your coffee mug. Add a sticker and it will be taken away. Inmates are desperate to have anything that is different. It is one way to try to hold on to your individuality. And the system will do almost anything to prevent that.

— Patrick, 51

TWO

The Little City

A S THE VAN MADE its way from county jail to Oakdale, Patrick felt both grateful and apprehensive. He was glad to be leaving county (all experienced cons said prison was better) but he was also worried about what might lie ahead. Would he have to fight anyone, or would the number of contacts he already had on the inside protect him? How much time would he actually spend behind bars?

Mostly, he wanted the deputy driving the van to stop so he could smoke a cigarette. There was no smoking inside Oakdale and he knew he would probably be there for a while. His thoughts were interrupted as the van pulled into the parking lot, the gates of the prison swung open and they were ushered into the compound.

Oakdale was basically a little city, with metal fences stretching around its 54-acre facility. A receiving dock abutted the back of one of the buildings, where the new prisoners alighted from the armored transport van. Correctional Officers in uniform smoked near the picnic table south of the visitor's entrance.

Patrick glanced at the razor wire, great coils topping and lying against the chain-link fence. The block-like buildings had narrow windows, and the glass was either frosted or so dirty that no one could see in or out. The cluster of buildings gave off an institutional vibe. The deputy checked his weapon and escorted Patrick, a short white man with long brown hair framing a weathered face, through a doorway into a cramped reception area.

As he entered the building, Patrick noticed a guard sitting behind an old wooden desk, beneath an observation post where two other Correctional Officers frowned down on their little parade. The room was small, containing only four chairs and two bookshelves lined with a raggedy selection of shredded paperbacks and dog-eared hardbacks, looking like they all dated back fifty years.

Oakdale houses 900 or so prisoners, including the general population of about 250 who make up the prison's supervised work crews. The inhabitants of this community, like those of any community, need adequate water, food, security, and medical care, so there's a power plant, a sprawling vegetable garden, a gymnasium, a pharmacy, and an industrial-sized laundry. There are medical units, GED classrooms, and rooms for religious services. It's the only prison in Iowa with a forensic psychiatric hospital, where mentally ill inmates receive care. In fact, the entire facility was built as a psychiatric hospital in 1969; it wasn't until 1984 that Oakdale assumed its status as classification center.[1]

'Classification center' means that every male prisoner who enters the Iowa correctional system is funneled through this place. Here, an inmate is classified according to crime, history, age, and behavior. They're assigned points to determine their status and where they'll end up—a minimum, medium or maximum-security facility somewhere across the state. Some will remain at Oakdale.

Initiating this process, the COs sorted through Patrick's property, allowing him to keep only his paperwork and his Bible. Everything else was thrown into a box, sealed up, and supposedly shipped to a friend's address. (Much later, after his release, Patrick told me he recovered only about a quarter of the items.) Once they entered all his pertinent information into the computer, the guards led him to a tiled area where he stripped off his county scrubs and showered with several other men who had just arrived.

They were then dressed in ragged blue jumpsuits and ordered to another room where an inmate barber shaved their facial hair, gave buzz cuts to those who wanted them, and their pictures were taken. This was the first time Patrick had been without a mustache for twenty years. He felt naked.

After a cursory exam by a doctor, his brief medical history was entered into the computer. He was asked some questions about alcohol and drug use and sexual experience by an intern, his blood was drawn, and then he set out with a little paper sack of toiletries, led by an inmate to another wing of the prison. The lettering on the door said "F Unit."

With a mechanical whine, the door clicked open. Patrick entered his new home, and began doing his time.

Tick. Tick. Tick. The minute hand of the analog clock on the wall of Oakdale's entry lobby inches slowly past 5. Leaning back in my chair, I cross my legs. Framed photos of white men—wardens past, the head of the Iowa Department of Corrections, the governor—stare down in pyramidal authority. Today, for some reason, our entry into the prison for rehearsal is delayed.

The fact is, time controls everything here. Either it's tightly regimented, or, so I'm told, there's so much you don't know what to do with it.

I imagine that when you're confined in one place, time's passage takes on an excruciating significance. An object (or a person) in motion tends to remain in motion. One at rest remains at rest. Staying in one place, "serving time," you might not get physically lost, but you can get left behind.

A philosopher once wrote that time is really only the mental measurement of movement.[2] In other words, it's all in your mind. I suppose insiders have plenty of time to wrap their heads around this concept.

"Time!" the activity coordinator finally steps forward and calls out.

"Listen up, everyone," Mary Cohen calls for our attention. It takes a few moments for the large group in the rehearsal room to settle down.

"I'm excited to get started today. For those who don't know," she says, "our choir is based on the principle of 'ubuntu.' Anyone know what 'ubuntu' means?"

One of the sopranos ventures: "We're all in it together?"

"That's right!" Mary exclaims. "It's a South African phrase meaning 'we are who we are because of other people, because of all of us together.' It's a beautiful idea, don't you think? I hope you'll think about that as you sing."

She steps onto the podium. "OK, let's start with some warm-ups. Feel your feet rooted in the floor. Stretch your arms, and roll your neck." Windmilling our arms from side to side, we suck in and expel deep breaths from our bellies. This may be one of the few opportunities insiders have all week to relax their bodies.

Mary sections the choir into three groups and we practice *solfege*, the do-re-mi building blocks of the Western chromatic scale. *Do re mi fa sol la ti do.* There are hand gestures symbolizing each note that Mary will ask us to memorize, though many of us find this challenging. She directs each group to hold a tone a third above the next group, and as our voices stack, a gorgeous harmony emerges.

In the early stages of the season we try out a number of choral pieces, which may or may not make their way into the final concert program. Now we open the score for "More Love," a traditional Shaker hymn. The sopranos begin the piece, and other sections join in. As we reach the end, Mary halts us and says, "OK, that's a good run-through. A few things to consider: enunciate your consonants! Try to end on the 'one', so that we have a crisp 't' at the end of the word 'not.' Otherwise we're all ending at different times, and it sounds like, I don't know, like popcorn. Let's take it from the bottom of page 4."

As we sing, a hollow 'L' shaped PVC pipe is being passed around the circle of the choir. When it reaches me, I hold one end to my ear and sing into the other end. The vibrations of my vocal cords resonate up through the pipe, take a sharp turn, enter my ear canal, pass the eardrums and ossicle bones, vibrating the strings of my cochlea. From there, it's a clear and strong shot into the brain. I can hear my own voice perfectly, allowing me to check my pitch. It's pretty amazing.

There's a real need for this kind of check. As the choir holds the opening note of the next piece, you can hear a sea of tones floating around the actual pitch, skewing sharp to flat. Somewhere in this room, pitches are being sung that are out of tune. Somewhere, an Oakdale singer is setting sail on his own bold, uncharted vocal course.

The range of musical skill in the choir is wide. Some members have years of experience; some have never sung a note before. Mary encourages us to listen to each other and bring our pitches into alignment, but that doesn't always work.

In the choir I sang with in high school, my fellow tenors and I had little compunction about correcting each other, or maybe mentioning to the director that some of us were struggling with the notes. But I hesitate to do that here. Most of these guys deal with judgment and criticism every day on the cellblock. Do I really want to correct someone and risk upsetting him? Or maybe I just haven't figured out how to do it in a way that honors the process. How vulnerable are we—outsiders as well as insiders—willing to allow ourselves to be?

Being in the choir is sometimes a little like juggling. Just as you think you've safely caught one ball, another comes whistling at you, and you've got to release the first one: you're adjusting to people's varying musical abilities; trying to connect with the people sitting next to you; maybe you're keeping in mind a big picture view of social justice; you're maintaining an acute awareness of your surroundings; and all the while trying to follow the score and sing. Sometimes it comes together beautifully; and sometimes we drop all the balls. A dynamic process, it can be a little overwhelming, for inside and outside singers both.

For example, today Mary asks for volunteers to stand up front and demonstrate how to clap a certain rhythm. The insider sitting in front of me, a guy I've been joking around with, grins and points surreptitiously over the top of his head, causing Mary to call on me. Everyone laughs.

I agree to go up, but joke, "OK, but let me throttle this guy first."

I say this because, well, I'm nervous about standing before this large group, and I want to acknowledge the situation, playfully.

But afterwards I think, hmmm, a joke about throttling someone…in prison…maybe not such a good idea?

As I said, this place can throw you off balance. How much more must it do so for an insider spending a significant portion of his life here?

I find it helps to get back to basics. Our orientation packet spells out the choir's collective goals: "To empower participants to embrace the joys of hard work for a meaningful purpose, build companionship rooted in sharing one's self and responding to others, gain confidence that each one of us can contribute to a greater good, and learn to honor who we are as individuals and as a community."[3] This is a great list, and it grounds me, once I get past my skittishness, in how to interact with others in the choir: sharing honestly (within the constraints) and keeping in mind the greater good. Come to think of it, it's not a bad prescription for life in general.

Before joining the OCC, I'd had little experience with prisons. I knew, intellectually, that criminal justice was an important issue, and that it was linked to other important issues like education, drug policy, racial justice, poverty, and mental health care. But embodying that knowledge—sinking into it and spending time and connecting with insiders—this was something new.

The atmosphere in prison is shaped and shaded by a constant sense of control; a feeling of helplessness can pervade the cellblock. This makes the central idea at the core of the choir—that every person, whether living in "normal" society or serving time inside, should have the opportunity to grow and find meaning—that much more powerful.

For these men, programs like the choir offer a chance to embrace an identity that's about more than just being a number in a cell. Though their lives are unfathomably complicated by their pasts, they, it seems, like anyone, long to have a voice.

I'm always surprised by what the men here know and can do. There are several professional musicians, highly trained and inspired, a man who wrote and published a book on prison life, two physicians. Of course, you can't get to know any one of us for very long before you get to see the broken place inside them, much sooner than you would on the street. Probably because one is disposed by the setting to pick up on such cues, not because daily life in America fails to provide a large supply of secretly broken men. We seem to be encouraged to think of ourselves as throwaway people. I dreamt last night of toilet paper sheets stamped with inmate numbers. Well, people here think that's pretty funny.

— Henry, 60

THREE

An Epidemic of Incarceration

THE UNITED STATES LOCKS up more people than any other country in the world. In 2017, U.S. federal and state prisons housed over 2 million people, or 1.6 percent of the adult population. We have five percent of the world's population and we've created 25 percent of the world's prisoners.

I've been learning a lot about prison issues since joining the choir, and many of the things I'm learning are disturbing. Thinking about the men incarcerated in Oakdale, I wonder: is there really so much more crime in the U.S. than in other countries? Or are we simply addicted to putting people away in greater and greater numbers, for longer and longer periods of time?

Actually, for much of the 20th century, the national incarceration rate hovered at only around one tenth of one percent of the population. And crime rates have been declining in recent years, depending on the type of crime. The violent crime rate peaked in the early '90s and has been going downhill since.[4]

So, why these soaring numbers of incarcerated?

According to researchers, the immediate causes of the incarceration epidemic include: the growth of drug laws which punished minor drug offenses with major prison time; "zero tolerance" policing; and mandatory sentencing laws, which have prevented judges from exercising discretion.

The 'three strikes' law, which sentences three-time committers of crimes to a life sentence, also means we are incarcerating more older adults than ever, often compounding time for crimes (strikes one and two) committed long ago.

Prosecutorial zeal plays a role as well. And common challenges for parolees, like missing appointments because of lack of transportation or housing, or being unable to pay fees, means thousands go back, pointlessly, to prison.[5]

But if crime rates are dropping as the prison population grows, doesn't this mean that putting people away curbs crime?

In fact, the opposite is true. A 2015 study from New York University School of Law's Brennan Center for Justice shows that prison played no role in plummeting crime rates over the past thirteen years. Rather, certain social factors can be shown to have affected the drop, including an aging population, changes in income, and decreased alcohol consumption. The study even warned that high levels of incarceration can increase future crime.[6]

As historian Robert Perkinson notes, "By herding together edgy individuals against their will and enacting daily rituals of subjection, even the best prisons tend to foster more conflict than cooperation."[7]

One problem facing criminal justice reform, another historian, Lawrence Friedman, writes, is that "a large segment of the population positively lusts to believe that criminality is raw, naked evil, the devil in human form. At the same time, millions seem to think that criminals are perhaps born that way... In both cases, rehabilitation, coddling, excuses, and psychological treatment seem a dangerous waste of time."[8]

The public's perception of those who commit crimes contributes greatly toward shaping public policy. And yet, once offenders are in prison, the public tends to forget about them. Perhaps we don't wish to be reminded of the fault lines—moral, economic, racial—that shift beneath our feet, threatening to disrupt the lives we have struggled to create.

I'm certainly not arguing that people who commit crimes should not be held accountable for them. They should. But as I learn more about the U.S. criminal justice system, I find I have more questions about how that might best be done.

The incarcerated include those awaiting trial in local and county jails, perhaps unable to pay their bail (about a quarter of the incarcerated population), those locked up in the extensive state systems (more than half), and those convicted of federal crimes who are placed in federal prisons.

Roughly eight percent of U.S. prisoners are housed in private, for-profit prisons (though there are no private facilities in Iowa). They're growing in number, cells of these prisons mutating and multiplying like biological cells. The insidious thing about for-profit prisons is that they need a full house to make a buck, and so they require municipalities in which they're built to keep arresting and incarcerating people. Meanwhile, their executives lobby Congress for tougher crime policies.

Private prisons tend to avoid taking sick and elderly inmates, since health care is a huge expense. One scholar studying Mississippi's system found that inmates in private prisons received many more conduct violations than those in government-run ones. This made it harder for them to get parole, and, on average, they served two to three more months of time, the implication being that private prisons work to hold on to their inmates longer.[9]

The 2005 annual report of one of the largest private prison operations, Corrections Corporation of America, notes, "The demand for our facilities and services could be adversely affected by the relaxation of enforcement efforts, leniency in conviction and sentencing practices or through the decriminalization of certain activities that are currently proscribed by our criminal laws."

Basically, the report warns about the possibility, as Adam Gopnik puts it, that someone might "turn off the spigot of convicted men."[10]

In rehearsal today, an insider makes his way down the rows of choir members and hands out copies of the soul tune, "Just My Imagination." Mary invites Karl, a white inside singer, and Karletta, an African American outside singer who's getting her PhD in sociology, to come to the front of the room for a duet.

Karl's voice is tinged with rhythm and blues intensity, while Karletta's spans a full gospel register. They get into a groove, their voices blending.

The choir leaps in, punctuating the melody: *Runnin' away with me!* A few folks bust some dance moves, stepping back and forth. The song seems oddly fitting, describing someone whose only interaction with the world takes place through a window, for whom imagination assumes primary importance.

Along with Otis Redding's "Sittin' on the Dock of the Bay," this song is part of an effort to expand our repertoire this semester. To bring da funk. Many of the pieces we've sung until now have fallen pretty squarely on the vanilla end of the spectrum. Taking on these two new songs grew out of a conversation Mary had with an inmate last year after he attended one of our concerts. She asked if he wanted to join the choir and he replied that one, he was a Buddhist, and couldn't relate to all the Christian songs, and two, why didn't we sing some Motown?

Our repertoire *has* tended toward more traditional choral music, the kind rooted in European church history. And leavened with musical numbers, and songs from other cultures, like the rousing Russian-language "Kalinka," a tune which brings to mind snowy steppes and fur-hatted Cossacks folding their arms and throwing their legs out in front of them to dance. These are all great. But throwing in some soul music, stretching ourselves, seems a good move, and might appeal to a broader audience.

As for the Buddhist inmate's other comment, about "all the Christian songs," it's true that some of the songs we sing are overtly Christian. Partly this is because so many insiders are Christian, and they're writing an increasing number of the songs we sing. But it's also because we're aiming for a positive tone, and those kinds of songs often spring from religious traditions.

I ask Amy, an outside singer friend who's Jewish, what she thinks about these Christian songs. She's not bothered, she says, since most of the songs we sing are, lyrically, more about values than specific doctrine. The important thing seems to be the feeling a song evokes, the attitude it engenders: we sing about what's brought us to this point in our lives, and the direction we now hope to take.

The practice of singing together, centered in the moment, can lead a group into liminal spaces, ready to be transformed. Anthropologists write about these kinds of ritual spaces all the time; Edith Turner used the word *communitas* to describe the state of collective joy that arises when each member of a group contributes to the group's creativity.[11]

But we also try not to avoid singing about life's harsh realities, the darkness with which many insiders are intimately acquainted, as epitomized by one insider's lyrics:

> *He swallowed comfort from a bottle that never seems to fill,*
> *Drew in comfort from a pipe that never warmed the chill.*
> *Took in comfort from a woman that never made him warm,*
> *Can he find some way, is there comfort to be had?*

Mary harbored a few reservations when she first brought the Otis Redding song to the choir.

"What do you think about singing 'Sittin' on the Dock of the Bay?'" she asked the insiders. "I'm worried that it might remind you guys of how hard it is to be in here, that you can't actually go sit by the bay?"

To which insider Reggie swiftly replied: "No, no, you're thinking about this all wrong. We want to celebrate those things, and remember them. It's not a burden to sing about that stuff."

In other words, the power of imagination and memory kindled by certain songs nourishes a tenuous link to the outside world. 'Dock of the Bay' becomes part of our repertoire, and later, in some of the writing exercises that augment the rehearsals (take-home writing prompts that allow singers to express their feelings about the choir), people wax enthusiastic about it.

"'Sittin' on the Dock of the Bay' is my favorite song we are doing," one person writes. "'Watching the tide roll away,' I compare that lyric to our slow waiting for that day when the tide rolls in, and I can walk through that gate, to freedom, and to my wife."

Another says: "My favorite's got to be 'Dock of the Bay.' I've sat on the beaches in Tampa looking out over the bay and the Gulf of Mexico, running from ghosts I'd left behind in Iowa and Nebraska, searching for the peace and tranquility that comes with the view. It was one of the most reflective times in my life. I had the chance to battle some of my demons and come out on top."

"To a lot of people, it may have just looked like I was wasting time. I might have been doing that, but it was in a good way."

Prison is a good place to think about time. Some things, like my sentence, seem eternal; but people seem ephemeral. They come and go all the time. You may like them, but when they go you hope never to see them again. And if you don't like them, or they have annoying habits, they are sure to be replaced by others just as disagreeable, or worse. "Do your own time and get out" is something you hear a lot, here. If you can ignore the rattle of headphones and the chatter of men doing business in stamps and tortillas, Pepsi and soups, prison gives you time to work on yourself.

— Henry

FOUR

A Liberating Thing

*T*HEN WE SAT ON *our own star and dreamed*—Van Morrison's bluesy
Irish brogue trips from the dashboard stereo of my car as I pull out
of the Oakdale parking lot—*of the way that we were and the way that we
wanted to be.*

When I joined the choir I think I wanted to re-experience the
impact that the music of someone like Morrison had on me when I
was young; his rhythmic sensibility, so free and swinging on a song
like "The Way Young Lovers Do," buoyed me through some dark
times. I love that song because of who I was when I first listened to
it, and what I needed from it—reassurance that it was OK to dream
of other ways of being.

There's no doubt that music can be a tonic, a touchstone, especially for
those who experience a lack of power. We know that civil rights activists
marching across the American South embraced song, not just as a welcome
accompaniment, but as a necessity. Singing set the pace, lifting people's
spirits in what must have been frightening, challenging circumstances,
and plugged people into their history.

Another example: when mortar shells whistled down on Sarajevo in
1992, and residents were forced to take cover in their homes for months
on end, local musician Vedran Smallovic risked his life by venturing into
a public square, setting up his cello and music stand, and performing
Albinoni's pensive "Adagio in G Major." His soulful playing pierced the

darkness, offering a glimmer of hope to his fellow citizens, music as balm and antidote to the barbarities of war.[12]

And this: in the latter half of the 20th century, a French scientist began research into the relationship of sound to the brain. Alfred Tomatis demonstrated that one function of the ear was, in effect, to charge the brain with energy by processing sound. His research, though controversial, paved the way for improving auditory function in autistic individuals.[13]

Tomatis was once invited to a Benedictine monastery, where monks traditionally spent hours a day singing and chanting in prayer. But the abbot at this particular monastery had decided to modernize things. He'd suspended the seven times-a-day singing of the *offices*—*compline, vespers, lauds*—considering them a time-wasting vestige from another era. As the days went by, the monks began to feel sluggish. Things were not going well down at the old monastery. So Alfred Tomatis was brought in, and he quickly figured out that the monks had previously used song-chant to, in a sense, recharge themselves. The suspension of this practice had undermined certain beneficial neurological and physiological effects. The monastics went back to their daily chants, and their energy rebounded.

Music heals, strengthening the human immune response. Jazz pianist Keith Jarrett was stricken with Chronic Fatigue Syndrome and could barely get out of bed for a year. It was partly the act of sitting down and picking out simple tunes at the piano that began to give him energy again, and somehow, mysteriously, contributed to reversing his illness. [14](As someone who deals with Chronic Fatigue, this story is especially inspiring to me.)

In his essay, "The Last Hippie," Oliver Sacks writes about a man with devastating amnesia who couldn't remember any new events in his life, but whose memory for music, and the experiences associated with it, remained intact.[15] Hearing songs from his youth, like The Grateful Dead's "Sugar Magnolia," allowed his past to open before him like a tableau. Song reached him as nothing else could, caressing a place beyond the conscious mind.

Science is beginning to understand the connections music creates for us. Listening to music we enjoy releases dopamine, one of the feel-good chemicals, into our bloodstream and brain. And singing with others sparks oxytocin, the bonding hormone, which the brain employs for building trust.

Singing slows the brain waves, leaving us feeling contented and peaceful. It helps us breathe more deeply and slowly, oxygenating the blood. It regulates blood pressure. Through the autonomic nervous system, the auditory nerve connects the inner ear to all muscles in the body; muscle strength and tone are thus affected by sound vibration.

It fascinates me to think about the indigenous Australians traversing the outback, chanting traditional song lines through the desert, following the route marked by their ancestors. Navigating long distances by repeating the words of songs describing the location of natural landmarks, they're not only singing the landscape into being, they're singing the journey into meaning.

Is there a culture that doesn't cherish singing? If so, it's a sad place I don't want to visit. Humans are hardwired to respond to music. The very cells of our bodies, vibrating with energy and light, shimmy in a constant rhythmic rhumba. Our hearts rebound with rhythm, blood pumping to a syncopated beat, as our breath ebbs and flows in dynamic cadence. We mark our lives in accented measures of time.

And before we're born, listening to our mothers' speech patterns, the sound of her voice vibrating down her spine and into our amniotic fluid, we're learning to harmonize with another human being.

The performance of music in American prisons has a long and fertile history. In 1947, for example, ethnomusicologist Alan Lomax recorded and released a number of penitentiary field recordings, such as 'Murderers' Home'—a collection of work songs and field hollers performed by inmates of the Mississippi State Penitentiary.

"These songs belong to the musical tradition which Africans brought to the New World," Lomax writes, "but they are also as American as the Mississippi River. They were born out of the very rock and earth of this country, as black hands broke the soil, moved, reformed it, and rivers of stinging sweat poured upon the land under the blazing heat of Southern skies, and are mounted upon the passion that this struggle with nature brought forth. They tell us the story of the slave gang, the sharecropper system, the lawless work camp, the chain gang, the pen."[16]

Blues and folk artist Lead Belly honed his musical chops while in prison, and he, too, was recorded by Alan Lomax.

And in the early 1950s, inside the walls of the Tennessee State Penitentiary, an African American doo-wop group called the Prisonaires was formed. Maybe the members had heard each other singing from their cells, or in the courtyard, and gravitated toward one another, urged on by other prisoners who sensed they shared something special. After some practice, the group became popular outside the pen, too, and were offered a recording contract with Sun Records (which recorded many Southern musical luminaries, including Jerry Lee Lewis and Roy Orbison). In 1953 they had a hit with "Just Walkin' in the Rain."[17]

The leader of the group, Johnny Bragg, had been inside since 1943 when, at the age of 17, he was convicted on six, quite likely trumped-up, charges of rape. In the band he was joined by two gospel singers, each doing 99 years for murder, and two new arrivals, in for larceny and involuntary manslaughter.

Their record sold 50,000 copies, and the group was let out of prison weekly to perform at the governor's mansion. The governor saw them as a model of positive rehabilitation. Even Elvis took an interest, reaching out to and befriending Bragg.

Fast forward a couple of decades. Americana singer Johnny Cash (another Sun Records alum) paid a number of visits to Folsom Prison, and later San Quentin, both in California, where he performed live concerts for the inmates to thunderous appreciation; these were recorded and became classic albums. Cash had developed an interest in prison issues while he was in the military. Throughout his career he performed for inmates all over the U.S., always unpaid, a passionate spokesperson for prisoners' rights.[18.]

And these days you can hear contemporary insider musical groups like "The Lady Lifers" perform songs with titles such as "This is Not My Home" on a TEDx program; their online videos reach wide audiences.[19]

This is all to say that all sorts of musical experiences have flourished in prisons: orchestras, dance bands, religious choirs; talent shows, guitar lessons, hillbilly bands; structured and tutored music education groups, many with paid directors. They're all examples of music animating the insider's soul, stoking dreams of other ways of being.

And it's not just music, but the arts in general, that do this important work. The film *Shakespeare Behind Bars* documents a project in which plays such as *Hamlet* and *The Tempest* are produced in Michigan and Kentucky prisons, with insiders playing all the roles. Hamlet's meditations on life and death assume extra layers of meaning when performed by a convicted murderer serving a life sentence. Director Curt Tofteland emphasizes that, on a practical level, theater can help insiders develop life skills and reintegrate back into society.[20]

Beyond this, he says, the expression of universal human experience through drama or song can have a transformative effect on insiders' lives.

Before arriving at the prison each week, I undertake a little ritual. I put my sheet music in order, and go over any challenging song passages sitting at my piano at home. I basically psyche myself up, setting the intention to be fully present with the people I'm about to spend time with. You have to muster an upbeat energy into this place. Other volunteers have told me they also try to let go of the day's distractions in order to remain *in the moment* with the guys. This can even be a bit freeing. The irony is not lost on us. Some volunteers may feel a measure of freedom leaving the world behind to enter the prison. But we'll be walking out again in two hours' time.

On a table at the front of the rehearsal room sits an institutional-sized water cooler and a tray of hard plastic cups. Everyone fills a cup with water on their way in and takes it to their seats. It's important to stay hydrated when you sing. You can place the cup underneath your chair but have to be careful not to kick it over, since there's a lot of standing and moving around during rehearsal.

Cups get kicked over anyway, and as the water spreads across the floor, it can be a test of how well you keep your cool. Apologize profusely, make a joke, fend off well-meaning jibes from those sitting next to you. Someone retrieves paper towels, and you mop up the mess so that no one slips in it. Mopping up your mess could, I suppose, be a metaphor for the work people are doing in here. Part of that means being mature enough, or vulnerable enough, to admit you made a mistake, and allowing those around you to forgive that mistake.

Today, the tray holds something different—cups made of soft flexible rubber, like Nerf cups, if there were such a thing. Rubber cups? I pick one up at the top and it squishes out of my hands.

I turn to one of the insiders. "What's with these cups?"

"Those are usually for the psych patients," he says. "They can't have anything they might hurt themselves with."

"I can't see how they might hurt themselves with a plastic cup."

He laughs, "Yeah, but there it is."

The cups must have been an anomaly, brought into the room by mistake, because after this rehearsal, during which we learn new gripping skills, we don't see them again.

AUTUMN

FIVE

Beauty Before Me

It's a lovely September day, the sun beaming down in warming benediction, the sky clear and startlingly blue. We make our way to the rehearsal room, mill around a bit, chatting, and then Mary calls us to attention. She begins the rehearsal by leading us in practicing a simple four-line chant that will open our concerts later in the season.

Beauty before me,
Beauty behind me,
Beauty above and below and all around.

Before singing the actual lyrics, though, Mary suggests we try something a little different. She asks everyone to choose a vowel sound and 'intone' it.

"Let's do some improvisation. Sing a vowel, like Ahh. Or Ooh," she says. "Then sing it on different pitches and harmonize with other people's pitches."

We give it a try. There are some tremendous female voices in the choir, and they fill the room with lilting upper register sound. You can feel the tones sculpt the space around us.

Mary urges us deeper into improvisational terrain. "Try some different vowel sounds, try some harmony and dissonance!" Voices inch their way upward in thirds and then stairstep back down to the middle range. I hear the man's voice next to me and follow it, and we engage in a game of vocal tag under the dome of sound.

"Now," Mary says, "bring some of the words from the song into your improvisation."

"Beeee-aaaa-uuuu-ttt-yyyyy"—the word stretches and hangs in the air above us, pulsating. I gaze around at people's faces—some are confused by the lack of structure, others seem joyfully lost in the spontaneity of the exercise.

Prison, with its razor wire, bad food, muted colors and fluorescent lights, is not generally thought of as either a beautiful, or a spontaneous, place. But here in the choir room, sometimes, both can be found. As the lyrics to another song we will sing put it, *I want to know if you can see the beauty, even when it's not pretty every day.* As we sing, we're shifting our reality, infusing it with something deeper than the environment typically offers.

This beauty is not necessarily a physical thing, though you can see it reflected in people's faces. I think it's more like a spark of energy that lights up the soul, a kind of manifestation of inner and outer congruence. When we human beings get harmonious, when we find, to use the phrase jazz musicians do to describe deep in-the-moment rightness, that we're *in the pocket,* it can be a beautiful thing.

After five minutes of building this sonic bridge, Mary steers us back around to the original tune and lyrics.

Beauty above and below and all around.

Our prelude of improvisation has charged the words with new meaning.

If this were a film, the camera might zoom in now to rest on the features of a man. Keith is a tall and lanky white guy, with an intelligent spark flickering in his eye. His voice carries energy, rising from deep baritone to a higher register; it reminds me of a sportscaster colorfully calling an inning-ending out during a series game. The camera pans across the choir and again settles on the man, as he puts this deep voice to good use practicing a solo for the Christmas song "You're a Mean One, Mr. Grinch," expressing our dismay at the Grinch's singular nastiness. After his solo, Keith smiles as he receives palm slaps and high fives from those sitting around him.

Not long before this, though, Keith was in a very different mood. He lay on his bunk, staring at the scar on his left arm. That scar had been there quite a while. He remembered the night he'd gotten it, long before he'd come to prison, following an argument he'd had with his live-in fiancée.

The disagreement had come down to this: she was supposed to either pursue her GED or get a job, and as long as she did either of those, Keith would continue to pay the bills. But she wasn't living up to her end of the deal, and he hadn't been happy working his tail off while she did nothing. The irony was that they had hoped that night would be a new beginning for the two of them. They had wanted to work things out. During the argument, though, things had gotten heated and she'd blurted out that she wished he was dead. Frustration gripped Keith. If that was how she felt, well, he'd show her. He took a knife and cut his arm. It wasn't a mortal wound, just enough to let her know he was serious.

As he sat in his cell now, Keith realized that he hadn't really cared then if he lived or died. In fact, for a long time as a young man, he'd been haunted by the feeling that he wouldn't make it past age 25. He'd accepted this, accepted the inevitability of his death, and gone on with life.

He didn't spend much time inside for the knife incident. Thirty days at the mental health center for an evaluation. Then forty days in county jail (he was charged with assault with a weapon) and he was out. It was later that he'd really screwed up.

The bell rang in the corridor outside his cell, jarring him from his reverie: time for dinner. That is, if you could call what the servers in the cafeteria slopped onto his tray, dinner. The meal was heavy on the carbs, the meat mostly gristle and fat. Didn't the cooks know how to use spices? It offended his sensibilities as a professional chef. He supposed it was better than bread and water. But he found himself dreaming about the kind of gourmet meals he used to create.

After dinner, he wandered back to his cell. It was small, and not particularly homey, but he made do. He had his own stainless steel toilet, while some inmates had to use a communal bathroom. He lay back and felt the thin mattress give under his weight.

When he'd first joined General Population at Oakdale, Keith had lived on T Unit, with eight men in a dorm-style room. After that, thanks to good behavior, he was moved to V Unit, had fewer men in his room, and could stay up until 11:30 p.m. on weekends. He also became eligible for more visits, which was great. And when a bed finally opened up on North Unit, he was moved into a two-man room!

These days, Keith viewed his situation philosophically. People made mistakes, but they could learn from them, he mused. Of course, there were some hopeless cases, where rehab just wouldn't take, but the majority of prisoners could rehabilitate if they chose to.

If you knew how to handle yourself, and didn't try to impress people, especially the wrong people, you could get by.

There are, of course, challenging moments in rehearsal. Today, as we practice "Breathe Holy Breath," one of the basses mistakenly sings on a rest, his voice blurting into the silence. Another singer, Ronald, disses him: "Nice work, dummy." A few men laugh; others seem uncomfortable with this insult.

Ronald is a young white inmate with short brown hair, a hawkish nose, and something to prove. He's constantly wisecracking, even when Mary is trying to explain something. This can give the rehearsal space the feel of a junior high classroom.

Some of the older men, like Everett and Burt, express their impatience with this cutting up. When I ask Burt one day where Ronald, who's missed a few rehearsals, has been, he replies, "Who cares? Good riddance!" It's clear that Burt has worked at achieving a measure of self-control and stability, and he's not happy to see the opposite tendency being flaunted.

There's also the new tenor, a young man whose neck is etched with an intricate web of tattoos. He's charming, but expresses a kind of swagger. A diffuse light in his eyes hints that he's rarely satisfied.

This guy brings an MP3 player to rehearsal, and surprisingly, plugs the buds into his ears and starts rocking out to other music while we're trying to rehearse.

The sound from the device can be heard, just barely, in our tenor section, though probably not in other sections, or by Mary. But he's sitting next to me, and it's pretty distracting. So I screw up my courage, tap his arm, smile, and say, "You know, this song we're practicing is kinda difficult, umm, even without any other noise."

The young man nods, laughs, and takes the earbuds out of his ears for a while. But the interaction makes me uneasy. I feel he needs to see that we're taking this choir business seriously, that we're trying to build something. Yet, even as I think this, my language—'he needs,' 'he should'—feels strange to me.

The contract between us is only one of human beings respecting a certain social order. Respect is one value the choir operates on. But it's one of those intangibles that you either get or you don't. People are free to act up. They're also free to leave the choir. On the other hand, maybe a little discipline helps you to experience some joy, the joy of creating something collectively. Self-discipline does seem to be a missing ingredient in many insiders' lives, especially early on in their incarceration.

I don't see the guy much after this, since he doesn't come regularly. When I do see him, he doesn't seem to have changed much, though of course this is just my subjective impression.

But he does keep coming, off and on, showing up, with an evident desire to be a part of things.

A new part of my practice is listening to Red Sox games on the radio. I'm not a big sports fan but there is something very meditative in the visualization involved. I guess it's a little like listening to music, which I don't get to do nearly often enough. I'm hoping to be able to spend some time with a guitar tomorrow.

— Henry

SIX

Origin Stories

PALE CLOUDS LIT BY arcs of sunlight sweep the sky. The air is crisp, though not enough to keep me from throwing off my jacket. Outside the University of Iowa library, students are making a beeline for their classes; others fling a Frisbee across a wide green lawn. I have an appointment a little later on campus, but for now I go down to the river. Standing on the bank, watching the eddies swirl downstream, my mind drifts to the memory of a time in my early teens, when I joined the Presbyterian Church youth choir—the Agapé Singers—in Arlington, Texas.

One reason I'm attracted to singing at Oakdale, I think, is because of the positive experiences I had with music when I was young. Another reason, perhaps, is that I was a somewhat mixed-up teenager. I can relate to people who are trying to straighten their own lives out.

Back then, my father, a small-town Iowa pastor, had decided to leave Iowa and the ministry, and we were starting our lives over in the suburbs of Dallas. It was a rough transition. Dad couldn't immediately find work, and I struggled to find my footing on the humid, wind-blasted school-yards of Texas.

There was one bright spot. The weekly Agapé Singers rehearsals offered something I wasn't able to find in other parts of my life: connection and creativity.

You had to give the director—a young dynamo named Michael Kemp—credit. Corralling a mob of unruly suburban teens into a competent musical ensemble was no small feat. He pushed us to attempt the most challenging pieces of music, and helped us grow as musicians. Eventually, we embarked on concert tours around the region.

Ours was no holy-roller church, more staid than slayed in the spirit, but we sang with gusto. *Elijah Rock, shout, shout! Elijah rock, comin' up, Lord. If I could I surely would, just stand on the rock where Moses stood. Elijah Rock, shout, shout!*

My fellow tenors and I may have waffled somewhat in our degree of religious belief; we may even have tried to crack each other up behind the choral loft wall during the sermon. But when it came time to sing, we stood, poured our hearts into the effort, and were rewarded. Singing offered a sense of beauty and accomplishment, and maybe, it succeeded in facilitating a kind of spiritual transcendence—taking us outside ourselves—where the service had not.

Texas *at large,* though, struck me as a place of bluster and old boy bravado, within whose bosom I did not feel welcome. I was gripped by dark moods, bullied as an outsider at school. My parents' marriage had been strained by the move and they didn't seem to have the energy to understand my struggles. And so as I morphed into a complicated teenager, a fissure began to grow in my psyche: Saturday nights and Sunday mornings tugged in opposite directions.

My best bud, David Slack, and I used to sneak off to a bar in a poor neighborhood of Fort Worth, called the New Blue Bird Lounge. There we danced to the house band, leaping across the dance floor sticky with spilled beer, and drowned our sorrows. I tended to overdo things, and Dave often had to shepherd me home safely.

But one thing I remember: the graying African American sax player, his beret slung low on his head, as he channeled his life force through brass and reed, playing the blues. You could almost sense him dipping his sax into the luminous well of being. You could hear in his playing the sadness of American history.

Such moments moved me, and, below the troubled surface of my own world, I sensed an ocean of possibility. Music performed from the heart, I was discovering, was a way of expressing an authentic self.

When I got a little older, I left Texas and traveled. I spent seven years in Asia, discovering there a rhythm with which to reframe my upbringing and my rebellion against it. Seeing other ways of being and doing stretched my brain and fired my imagination. I learned to meditate, which helped channel my energy in a positive direction.

And in most of the places I visited I noticed how the simple act of singing filled people's hearts, how collective music-making connects us to each other and to something greater than ourselves.

I see the songs we sing in the Oakdale Community Choir now in a similar light. They also hold out powerful messages of hope. The intentions we bring to the rehearsal room—mutual support, a commitment to expressing deeper human energies—allow us all, insider or outsider, healthy or broken, shy or gregarious, to transcend a little.

They allow us to free ourselves, if only for a moment, from the thorny bonds of the past.

⚜

Mary Cohen's office is on the second floor of a brick university building, not far from the river. She invites me to sit at a table in the corner. Books line the walls and lie open on her desk, passages marked. Several department colleagues pop their heads through the door and say hello from time to time.

I'd like to know more about the Oakdale Choir's origin story, the encounters and connections that led to its creation. Cohen leans back in her chair and considers the question.

In the early 2000s, she tells me, she was living in Kansas City, working as an elementary school music teacher. She'd heard something about a choir being organized in a local prison, combining the voices of community volunteers and the incarcerated. One Sunday morning, relaxing over the newspaper, she noticed a concert listing for this choir: the East Hill Singers, at Lansing, the largest male facility in Kansas.

"Hmm. Looks interesting." She decided to attend.

Light streamed in through stained glass windows at the local Lutheran church, as volunteers in short-sleeve pastel colored shirts and inmates in prison blues filed into the makeshift performance space. (Inmates had been allowed out of prison for this special occasion). Cohen watched as the conductor strolled to the front of the sanctuary, raised her hands, and with a flourish brought the singers in on the first number.

They sang Schubert's "Holy, Holy, Holy," and other songs. Between pieces, the men spoke about their lives, and about how they were changing. Cohen checked out a display of prisoner art that filled the church's vestibule—watercolors, note cards, pencil sketches, poetry. She was moved.

She learned that the director, Elvera Voth, a former choral director, had wanted to get involved in some sort of social justice work following her retirement. At age 70, Voth dreamed of teaching the incarcerated to sing. The warden at Lansing, David McKune, thought it was a crazy idea, but told her, "Go ahead and try." He eventually became one of her biggest supporters.

Voth describes how some of the prisoners had never sung before at all: "At first they looked stunned. I think some couldn't read words, let alone music." She developed a technique to help these singers. When a singer had trouble matching a pitch on the piano, she wouldn't hit the key over and over. Instead, she let him sing whatever pitch he wanted and then matched it on the piano. *Oh, is that how it feels?*[21]

Hearing Voth's stories, a bulb flickered on for Cohen. She'd thought about pursuing a PhD in music education, and now, things seemed to be aligning. She made a decision: to research prison choirs for her doctoral work.

Several basic questions would stand at the heart of this research. First, did singing in a choir offer opportunities for transformational experiences, for both inmates and volunteers? And, as someone who practiced yoga and other movement practices, Cohen was interested in the somatic aspect of prison choirs, and wanted to know how bodily movement could engage singers and enrich their experience.

Perhaps typical inmate behaviors—the need for instant gratification, a lack of personal and social responsibility, and weakly developed social skills—might be addressed, even modified to some degree, through the discipline of singing in a choir?[22]

These were big questions, but inside singers she interviewed hinted at the answer: "Paying attention to detail was a new experience for me. And I find that it now spills over to other areas of my life."

Said another, "Trust and reliance on other people is hard to come by in prison. But here with each other and with the volunteer singers, we know that we can relax and enjoy each other. Most important, I've learned to trust myself."

And, "In prison you have a tendency to hang around your own ethnic group. Coming to something like this you see those barriers disappear."[23]

It was likely that volunteers benefitted, too, as they became more aware of prison issues and began to perceive the insiders as more than just numbers. I know I did.

Patrick surveyed his surroundings. He'd been assigned a lower bunk and he sat down and looked around the cell. Besides the two metal bunks with thin mattresses, there was a steel toilet/sink combination, a metal desktop with a steel stool that swung out from the wall, and absolutely nothing else. The room was about eight feet by eight feet, but one of the corners had been walled up behind the toilet, making it even smaller. A narrow window rose behind the bunks, but Patrick could see nothing through it.

The walls were grimy, studded with unknown substances that seemed to have become one with the concrete. Water stains smeared the ceiling and in some places, the paint was peeling from walls and floor; in others it was totally worn away. Crude graffiti was splotched here and there, along with the occasional name or insult. These were etched deep into the paint, probably with a nail or a screw from somewhere.

Patrick opened his bag. Inside were two envelopes, a pencil, some sheets of notebook paper, a stubby toothbrush, a clear tube of toothpaste, a tiny bar of soap, and a little stick of deodorant with no discernible odor. The room itself had an odor, though—a miasma of urine, sweat, farts, and blood. Overlying all was the sharp tang of bleach.

He tried flushing the toilet and pushing the buttons on the sink, which allowed a lukewarm stream of water to arch toward the drain for about four seconds before shutting off automatically. Standing up, he looked through the slit window in his cell door. This one you could see through, sort of. He noticed tables in the day area where an inmate was laying out sheets of paper. Then he sat back down on the edge of his bed and waited, wondering if he would get bedding or if he was to sleep on a bare mattress.

As if in answer to his thought, the door hummed and then clicked open. He was given two sheets and a thin blanket. After making his bed, he sat at the table, filled out forms and wrote a letter to a Mr. Zeb.

Mr. Zeb must have received many such letters by now. Patrick was given a sample printed letter and told to copy it word for word, writing in cursive, which he hadn't used since freshman year of high school. When he finished, he was told to copy it again, this time printing the text. At this point he realized he was giving the DOC handwriting samples for future use.

Shortly after, he and his unit were escorted to the chow hall where unsmiling COs pointed them to their seats and watched their every move. The food was okay, much better than it had been in county jail, but they were only given 15 minutes to eat. Those who didn't finish were forced to throw the rest away. He learned other rules: you couldn't talk to anyone at another table, you couldn't give or take food from anyone not at your table, and people at your table weren't shy about asking for *your* food! A generous person could easily starve.

The rest of that day was spent shuttling between his cell and health services. In the afternoon he got a cellmate, a man in on a ten-year drug sentence. Patrick knew that longer sentences carried status and his own 25-year sentence earned him some respect. But it didn't stop his roomie from complaining. People with two- or five-year sentences tended to complain more than those with longer ones, Patrick had noticed. After spending nine years of his life locked up, Patrick still hadn't figured that one out.

Mary Cohen soon became the director of a men's choir at Osawatomie Therapeutic Community Facility in Kansas, a prison focused on changing addictive behaviors through cognitive restructuring. She enjoyed getting to know the inmates, and learning about their lives inside. When she led them in their first enunciating warm-up—"Diction is done with the tip of the tongue and the teeth!"—one inmate asked, "What if you don't have any teeth?" Everyone laughed.

In her PhD work, she began constructing a theory of choral singing pedagogy based on Christopher Small's concept of "musicking."

Small, a New Zealand-born musician and educator, believed that music, far from being a static object, was an action, a communal activity. He coined the term "musicking" to describe this active quality. Musical meaning, he wrote, is drawn from both the sound and the social experiences of music making—relationships among sounds and people, and the processes of exploring, affirming, and celebrating those relationships.[24]

According to Small, "to music" is to take part in any capacity in a musical performance—performing, listening, rehearsing, practicing, writing, or dancing. Even the guy selling tickets at the concert hall door participates in this communal aspect.

Cohen advanced her dissertation during this period. (One inside singer would often ask her, "Mary, how's your dysentery going?") After earning her PhD in 2007 and taking a position at the University of Iowa, she founded the Oakdale choir in 2009. And she began working to connect with an international community of prison music educators, rooted in a relatively new approach to criminal justice reform.

This approach, known as "restorative justice," focuses on the process of accountability for those who have committed crimes, helping them understand the impact their behavior has had on others, and responding to and repairing that harm. (A related approach, "transformative justice," focusing on changing the social conditions that lead to crime and imprisonment, is also becoming influential.)

Iowa attorney Bruce Kittle, who has served as a prison chaplain, describes restorative justice this way: "The community is not left on the sidelines to watch, but invited to be actively involved in their neighborhoods and communities in not only responding to crime, but expressing community values and creating resources and opportunities that eventually result in the reduction of crime."[25]

Buzz Alexander writes about a remarkable event he witnessed in the film "Sentencing Circles—Traditional Justice Reborn" epitomizing this approach. In a Canadian indigenous community, elders gathered for a sentencing circle. They apologized to the wayward youth whose sentence they were determining. We did something wrong in raising you, they said, or you would not be standing here before us.[26]

Such awareness of the way the offender is connected to the community is at the heart of restorative justice, the understanding that, when violence is perpetrated, the community itself frays. Achieving justice means offering understanding, healing, and restoration for all involved. This, of course, includes the victim. A crucial aspect of restorative justice lies in supporting crime victims and their needs.

"The engaged and inclusive process itself transforms people," Bruce Kittle adds, "and when people are transformed, they in turn transform their communities and, eventually, the system. This is not 'top down' but a process that builds from the foundation of a community up."

Cohen saw choral music as a way to put some of these values into practice. By transmuting life stories into music, she felt inmates could develop more empathy and a broadened perspective of the harm they'd inflicted. She writes, "Other aspects of restorative practices evident [in music programs] include problem-solving skills, conflict transformation, tools for improved relationships with family members, personal growth, self-esteem, respect, and strengthened communities."[27]

The academic literature suggested great things. One researcher noted that music programs in prisons could lead to restorative justice practices even when nested inside systems that are primarily retributive. Another reported that female Israeli prisoners participating in a choir developed listening and breathing skills that helped reduce tension. They learned to modulate their voices in order to communicate more respectfully, engaged in delayed gratification, and developed improved self-esteem.

There was one key aspect of restorative justice, however, that the scope of these choirs did not at first seem to allow for—interaction between victim and perpetrator.

But as part of a general restorative justice approach—encouraging people to become accountable, and acknowledging all parties' basic humanity—it was a good start.

⸻

I have an MS in Electrical Engineering. On the outside, my thing was robots—I've been interested in them for as long as I can remember. My focus was always on humanoid androids, though I also thought about creating robot pets. I want to build companion robots that can interact with humans, using easy kits that students can assemble. I was starting a robot business when I got sent to prison.

— Jackson

SEVEN

Dangerous Place

WHEN I RETURN HOME from choir on Tuesday evenings, prison vibes often linger around the edges of my consciousness. Usually I have dinner with Lois. We watch the news or read, talk about the choir a bit, and then migrate toward sleep. But sometimes I lie awake, a bit keyed up, wondering what things are like for the inside singers after they head back to their cells. Outsiders don't see much of the insiders' daily lives. But there are things I'm beginning to understand.

Prisons are crowded, noisy places. There's little privacy, and you're living with others who may be unpredictable or violent. Prison designers, as researcher Victor Hassine puts it, have developed "a precise and universal alphabet of fear that is carefully assembled and arranged—bricks, steel, uniforms, colors, odors, shapes and management style"—in order to control the conduct of prison populations.[28]

I imagine (and conversations with inmates confirm) great uncertainty living on the cellblock. Buttons get pushed; expressing your feelings is not encouraged. People in prison live under the threat of being "punked out," becoming the sexual slave of another inmate. The state of Iowa has taken steps to combat such occurrences, through implementation of the federal Prison Rape Education Act, but it still happens.[29]

I imagine (and research shows) that inmates struggle with anxiety when they think about life after prison. They worry about the financial obligations that wait for them on the outside. It won't be easy to find good employment saddled with a criminal record.

An insider has lost a lot—income, relationships, social status. He or she likely struggles with a sense of identity. What does it mean to no longer be a free citizen? Who am I, in this place?

Young people in prison often grapple with an alphabet soup of psychological issues—Conduct Disorder, Oppositional Defiant Disorder, Attention Deficit and Hyperactivity Disorder. Many have intellectual disabilities. Only three percent of prisoners were classified as proficient in reading and writing in a National Center for Education Statistics literacy assessment in 2003.[30]

Getting old in prison is no cakewalk, either. Simple actions, like climbing to a top bunk, become extremely difficult. Mobility aids for older adults, such as handicapped toilets and handrails, don't exist in many prisons. Over the course of several years I have watched some choir members falter into older age; worry lines crease their faces, hips and knees give out, canes and wheelchairs show up increasingly in rehearsal.

I also know, thanks to research done by the Prison Policy Initiative, that people who go to prison are usually poor.[31] They're often unable to afford good legal representation, and usually don't know their options. Often, laws are slanted in favor of the well-to-do. "Law protects power and property," Lawrence Friedman writes, "safeguards wealth, and perpetuates the subordinate status of the people on the bottom."[32]

For some people, it was the sale or possession of marijuana that landed them inside. When it comes to weed, there's a disproportionate conviction rate for young people of color, and possession of even small amounts of a substance that is arguably less dangerous than alcohol can mean long sentences and shattered lives.

For others, it was the decidedly more dangerous meth that pulled them astray. You may have seen the TV series *Breaking Bad*, which offers a glimpse into the devastating nature of methamphetamine addiction, an addiction which spurs uncontrollable urges and compels a user to do anything for the next hit, then consigns them to a toothless, shambling non-future. For the dealer, there's the lure of an obscene amount of money to be made.

Meth addiction continues to spread in the heartland, collateral damage, some would say, of dying rural economies that languish in the shadow of corporate agribiz. Addiction to heavily-marketed opiodes, another outgrowth of social and economic hard times, is also growing.

Finally, the degree of trauma people in prison have faced can be astonishing. Stories of absent, alcoholic or emotionally abusive parents are common. There's an official checklist for causes of trauma, and most prisoners can tick off many of these points. Drugs. Witnessing a homicide. Witnessing or experiencing a natural disaster. Witnessing sexual abuse. Being sexually abused. Check, check, check.

Such trauma has been shown to play a role in shaping criminal behavior. So-called "adverse childhood events" can actually change the cellular structure of the brain. Says UK researcher Paul Renn, "Research findings relating to young offenders show a history of maltreatment and loss in up to 90 percent of the sample population."[33]

Keith wandered over to the main corridor. He liked to spend time browsing the canteen, where you could purchase items ranging from instant coffee to ramen noodles, shoes to playing cards, shirts to toothpaste, and deodorant to radios.

Today he bought some cheese spread and crackers and walked back to his cell. Lying on his bed, munching on the crackers, he let his mind wander.

His mother and father had divorced when he was young, and his mother moved her children—Keith and an older brother and sister—back to Nebraska after a stint in North Carolina. She earned a degree in computer programming and when Keith was in first grade, they moved to Grinnell, Iowa, where she took a job at Grinnell Mutual Reinsurance Company.

Grinnell is a city of under 10,000. Known for its progressive liberal arts college, it's in other ways a typical Midwestern town. Exit the interstate onto the main drag, and you'll pass, somewhat predictably, a Walmart, an auto parts store, a Chinese restaurant, and a Pizza Hut. Keith attended school there through the 12th grade.

He thought of the speech therapy class he'd been placed into in elementary school, having had difficulty pronouncing the sounds 's' and 'sh,' as well as 'r.' It was probably something about that speech impediment that sparked his passion for writing. But, he'd improved and even won a contest; he remembered his presentation, portraying a garbage collector (poor speech) and a businessman (good speech), implying that proper diction could improve your life.

Early on, he wanted to be a teacher, and had hopes of attending Concordia University. Poetry was his passion. He hesitated to show his work to others, but when a friend needed lyrics for songs he was writing, Keith shared a poem with him. The friend raved, and Keith began to feel more comfortable with this whole putting-your-work-out-there business.

But, there had also been summers like the one when he turned 14. He was arrested twice for shoplifting—once for CDs, once for adult magazines. Wasn't that also the year that he and three of his friends had been hauled in for joyriding and possession of alcohol? For that, he'd been placed on probation for two years.

Keith smiled to himself; he'd made it through the probation period, but not because he'd behaved. He just never got caught. When was his next brush with the law? At 17, he pled guilty to marijuana possession. And at 18, he was arrested again for joyriding. After a short jail term sentence, he was placed on probation again.

A thin ray of light filtered into his cell. Keith squinted, and shifted his position on the bunk.

It wasn't peer pressure that motivated his drug use, he mused, but it certainly hadn't deterred him either. Around the time he turned 13, he and his closest friends tried marijuana for the first time. He liked the expansive feeling it gave him, and in search of other highs, he tried other, harder drugs. LSD offered a more cosmic experience, opening the doors of perception and all that. But he never experienced the graphic hallucinations some people said they had. He kept searching.

Methamphetamines were intense. Things seemed to last longer, and he never got tired. He could party, write poetry, and get his chores done without having to sacrifice anything. His drug use had never been only about how a drug made him feel. If that were the case, he would probably have done more of the other drugs. Heroin was by far the best feeling, but his productivity on heroin wasn't the greatest.

Keith thought of the many jobs he'd held during that time; the one he'd loved most was cooking. He took a job at the Iowa Machine Shed, a popular restaurant in Des Moines, and moved up the ladder rapidly from line cook to prep cook to executive chef. He began to teach a monthly cooking class, did cooking demos at the state fair and even appeared as a chef on morning TV shows. He was making good money but he was also becoming highly stressed.

He married his girlfriend in 2005. They divorced within two years. Keith took the blame for things falling apart. He had let Catherine assume he was cheating on her rather than tell her he was on a country road shooting meth into his veins. By age 21, he'd been drinking and smoking marijuana regularly for more than five years, and using cocaine and meth, as well. The more he felt his marriage slipping into disarray and his work life becoming difficult, the more he used.

Drugs had also been a stimulus for his creativity—the clichéd dark artist thing. On top of this, meth allowed him to go on cruise control, erasing certain feelings. When he was stressed out or thinking about his absent father, marijuana might ease his pain. But with meth, his problems disappeared entirely.

Working twelve hours a day had left him with little time for himself. Simply put, meth provided him with more time.

Of course, it would later steal all of that time back, and then some.

The activity coordinator stares at us as we file into the waiting area. His face is grim.

Something happened the previous week. I was home sick, but I learned about it when Mary sent out an email reminding us to stick together while entering and leaving the rehearsal room. Apparently, the line of volunteers had gotten stretched thin when a few people delayed leaving the choir room after rehearsal, no doubt deep in conversation with inside singers. The coordinator had lost sight of some of the volunteers and was worried that something might happen to them.

I didn't think much about this. We often passed non-choir inmates in the hall, nodding to them and either getting a nod back or no eye contact at all. Positive interactions with insider choir members had led many outsiders to feel well disposed toward the other men we encountered in the halls. Most of us moved through these corridors not with a sense of fear or suspicion, but with a hopeful desire to connect.

But this week the coordinator stops us before we leave.

"I just want to say something," he begins. "The reason I got so upset last week is, this is a dangerous place! Some of these guys in the hallway, they're in for murder, or rape, what have you! They may be serving a life sentence. So they've got nothing to lose. They're just waiting for a chance to jump out and grope one of the females, or worse." He becomes animated, a sense of distrust radiating from his words.

"You guys don't know," he goes on. "Anything can happen. It does happen. You can never let your guard down in a prison. Never. And I'm responsible for your safety."

It's true, during orientation, we'd been warned that prisoners were good at manipulation. We'd been reminded that we weren't there to be their friends, only to sing next to them. In short, we were to exercise caution, and not get too close.

But I wonder if he's being a bit alarmist. Although we occasionally hear stories about prisoners who act out or act up, most of the insiders seem keen to continue having us visit, and they regulate their behavior accordingly.

But it's complicated, because there *are* dangerous people in prison, in *this* prison.

Karla Miller, who works as a trauma therapist and counselor with sex offenders at Oakdale, says her work has reinforced for her the sense that inmates can be opportunists.

She recalls one such person she met, whose eyes were "like slate, closed down, with a lack of empathy or warmth. He talked about hitting a deer with his car, and he was genuinely sad. But he couldn't make that connection to human beings."

She also worked with a minister who had abused kids. "He had even won an award for his work with children. After being discovered as an abuser, he was sent to prison. I asked him, how do you justify your behavior? 'Oh, that's easy. This is my day job and this is my private life.' He had this amazing ability to compartmentalize. He was a pillar of the community, giving him access, and people couldn't believe that he could be a bad guy."

Some of these people are sociopaths, she believes, those who will abuse anyone they come in contact with. (Later, Oakdale's chief physician will tell me he doesn't much like the term 'sociopath.' If true sociopaths exist, he says, they're few and far between.)

Nevertheless, the harm done to victims—long lasting and traumatic—hovers over many of these cases. And the crimes are serious. You can see the crimes that have landed people in prison on the Iowa Government Data website: Drug trafficking. Drug possession. Murder/manslaughter. OWI. Burglary. Weapons. Assault. Vandalism. Sex Crimes.[34]

Information supplied by Bruce Kittle notes that crime victims are subject to impact in four major areas: physical (trauma to body, bruises, broken bones, cuts, burns, scars, ulcer, fatigue, HIV); emotional (fear, anger, hopelessness, insecurity, guilt, shame, confusion, depression); psychological (paranoia, social isolation, inability to sleep, depression, nightmares, inability to feel clean); and financial (personal expenses, loss of wages, insurance deductibles, law enforcement costs, medical costs, funeral costs). They also have concerns about their safety, and about being believed. Long-term reactions may include PTSD.[35]

Jonna Williams-Kasprzak was the victim of a brutal sexual assault when she was thirteen, abducted in broad daylight by a repeat offender who was

high. She's now 37. I was put in contact with her through the Iowa Office
of Victim Services. She bristles at the idea of calling what offenders have
done 'mistakes.'

"Although in some instances what they've done are mistakes," she says,
"in many cases that word is not broad enough to encompass the impact
a crime has. My family suffered as well. And my daughter now continues
to feel the effects of the crime." She resists the idea that offenders landed
in prison simply because of their difficult life experiences, instead of the
consequences of their choices.

All the things that an inmate is provided with, Williams-Kasprzak says,
like medical care, the provision of food and shelter, even opportunities
to learn to sing, are things that victims often have to pay for as a result
of the crime committed against them. And, she says, the Crime Victim
Assistance Fund is limited.

"While I do value offender rehabilitation and can absolutely see the
benefit for it individually and for a community, it's noteworthy that I pay
for my own rehabilitation. I pay for my recovery from the sexual assault.
For every opportunity offered to offenders, I want to ask, are those same
opportunities offered to victims? I have to advocate for myself for things
the average person would never consider."

She also wonders about the emphasis on 'second chances' for offenders.
"I wonder about their victim, and whether *they* have second chances," she
says. "Dead victims don't get second chances."

"Still," she continues, "the one thing I did always hope for in my case is that
the offender did something to be productive and constructive and he didn't
just sit in prison watching TV. I hoped he did something that gave back."

It's vitally important to recognize victim experiences in the overall
criminal justice story. And Karla Miller reminds me that many inmates
are still prone to opportunistic thinking. She sees those who can and have
changed, but also those with more selfish tendencies.

I'll recount more of my conversation with Miller later in the book.
But her words and those of victims like Williams-Kasprzak add to the
refrain of warnings that lodge in the back of my mind: These men have
committed crimes. Some of them are violent. Some have caused a lot of
pain. Their victims have to live with that pain. There's a reason they're in
prison. Don't get too chummy.

This is all true.

And yet, as volunteers in the choir, we often hold two contradictory ideas
in our minds at the same time. What I'm learning as I enter the prison each

week and do more research on prison issues, is that prisoners, like members of any group, are not all the same. Each has an individual trajectory. Many are sincere in their desire to atone for their crimes, start over, and better their lives. They may need to reach a new level of self-awareness before they can turn in a different direction. And that can take time.

And sure, some will remain stuck, mired, in self-pity, self-aggrandizement, or self-ignorance. Maybe some *are* opportunistic, and we choir volunteers are being manipulated by them. It can be difficult to know who is genuinely remorseful. Mary Cohen reminds the outsiders that we don't want to foster an environment in which men who are prone to self-pity are allowed to wallow in it. And always, we need to remember the struggles of the victims.

But should we let the *possibility* of violence, or manipulation, or resistance to change—the fact that some inmates are trouble—affect how we interact with those many who *are* trying to better themselves? Impose a one-size-fits-all presumption upon these guys out of an abundance of caution? Forego taking the risk of connecting, out of fear?

I don't think so.

As for difficult people being our teachers, you got that right. It gets pretty hairy sometimes. The assumption is that a little more self-knowledge might have kept us out of prison in the first place, and a lot more wouldn't hurt. One wants to believe that the pain, confusion, grief are worthwhile, that a form of redemption is possible, that one can learn to live in a way that is not harmful. That's the plan anyway. I'm determined to make it work in my case.

— Henry

EIGHT

Tricky

DAH DAH DAT DAH dah... DAT! Dah dah DAT dah dah... DAT!
Mary is standing in front of us and clapping a rhythm. We're supposed to follow her lead—clap this rhythm out with our hands and beat it against our thighs. But it's highly syncopated, and she jumps into it so casually, I have no idea what's going on. Somehow I've missed the context for it. Maybe she's following up on an exercise she started when I was absent. I look around. I can tell some of the other tenors feel a bit at sea, too.

There are moments like this, early in the season, when we're trying to create something, but we don't yet know what we're doing, and the notes don't line up as they're supposed to. We sound raggedy. The rhythm is off.

Following a musical conductor under any circumstances can be tricky. And here, many members have never done anything like it before. The same goes for reading a musical score—there are clefs and signature signs and tempo instructions to interpret, sometimes in Italian or Latin. Repeats and codas. And how many of us know how to breathe from the, what is it, diaphragm?

When you stop to think about it, the very process of hitting a musical pitch is mysterious. Your eye sees a squiggle on a page, and this somehow translates into a specific sound in your brain, which your voice then aims to express. But it doesn't always land where it should. Having the piano accompanist play the pitch helps. And the good thing about a choir is that you've got others to lean on, who can help cover up your mistakes.

My point is, we're all learning a lot, we're eking our way through often unfamiliar territory, and there are plenty of challenges. Because of this, in the free moments following rehearsal, Mary often fields comments (and complaints) that well up like floodwaters.

One man declares, "I don't like the other insiders' original songs—they're too depressing."

Another says, "I'd like to sing more upbeat songs in the winter months."

A man wonders why we have to practice the same song over and over—he just wants to sing a song once and move on.

These challenges are part of the group's history. In the early days, OCC members would read and discuss excerpts of books, like Bo Lozoff's *We're All Doing Time*. (Lozoff ran one of the first successful prison meditation programs in the U.S.) But conservative Christians in the choir, upset by the book's unorthodox spirituality, protested its use.

Another time, an insider wrote lyrics for a song and asked Mary to set these words to music. But after we rehearsed the song, an anonymous note appeared mysteriously on Mary's podium, "X does not like the music to this song."

And once, when she set an insider's lyrics to music, the experience apparently went to the man's head. Some of the men told Mary they were tired of the song, because it had "turned the composer into a monster."

Mary does her best to listen to these complaints, and explain why it is we're doing certain things ("I could do a lot better about explaining things up front," she tells me), or ask the men to be patient as we work through a challenging season.

Basically, we try not to sweat the small stuff. And part of the choir's process is learning that, even as we're committing to tackling a big project, it's all small stuff. Besides, there's plenty of time to improve. That's really what this is all about—starting from scratch, and slowly getting better and better.

Now, as we begin the next song, several tenors gravitate toward singing the melody, not the tenor part. That this is not the point in four-part choral singing doesn't seem to bother them.

Daniel Craig, the new Deputy Director of Institutional Operations for the Iowa Department of Corrections (DOC) was until recently the warden at Oakdale. I remember him attending our concerts, a well-dressed, personable man standing at the back of the gym.

Plenty of negative impressions exist about prison wardens. Daniel Bergner's book *God of the Rodeo*, for example, portrays the warden of Angola Correctional Facility in Louisiana as a man who pretends to be concerned about his wards, but who really is just in it for himself.[36] Then, of course, there's the unimaginably cruel 'boss man' in the film *Cool Hand Luke*.

I have to say, though, that the wardens I've encountered in the Iowa system strike me as thoughtful and dedicated.

Craig welcomes me into his office at the DOC administrative building, a bureaucratic block across from the impressive gold-domed state capitol in Des Moines. He's friendly, perhaps a bit distracted with his new duties. But he remembers the choir fondly.

"You're walking down a prison corridor one evening, and you hear, echoing down the hall, the blended tones of fifty voices. It's calming," he says. "Peaceful. Beautiful. Almost like being in church."

Craig attended every concert that took place under his watch and observed the impact the choir had not only on insiders, but on community members as well, receiving many letters from guests impressed with the quality of the program.

For him, the benefits of the choir far outweighed the need to provide additional security. Of course, he had concerns about how much it would cost—everything has to be managed within budget constraints. A large number of visitors had to be checked in for concerts, which meant reassigning officers. Initially, there was some staff resistance. Over time, though, that resistance lessened, as staff members came to appreciate the atmosphere the choir created.

Another retired prison superintendent (from Minnesota Correctional Facility in Red Wing), Otis Zanders, echoes this thought. While prison safety has to be a priority, Zanders, quoted in the article "Finding Freedom Through Song," believes "Good programming makes good security. If the offenders buy in to the program, they police themselves."[37]

"These are men in survival mode," Zanders goes on. "We're looking for ways to move them up Maslow's Hierarchy of Needs to self-actualization." (He's referring to psychologist Abraham Maslow, who postulated a hierarchy of human needs, ranging from basic physical ones on up to trust, relationship, and self-understanding).

Being imprisoned *is* the punishment, Craig reminds me. There's no need to intensify the experience. With that in mind, what do you do for prisoners once they're inside? You focus, Craig says, on preparing them for reentry into society. You identify risk issues and treatment needs through assessment, and you use programming to change thinking. The emphasis is on changes in behavior.

And you can't just boot them out the door when they're released, he says; they'll need a well-structured plan, support systems, therapy, and job opportunities. There may also be substance abuse or sex offender issues to deal with.

"Ninety-five percent of them will go back out to become our neighbors again," Craig says. "We want them to be neighbors you can trust with family and friends. They'll need skills to survive, programming to help them make the right choices. Volunteer activities like the choir are a complement to that, to help improve their lives."

Actually, several prisoners I've spoken with have mixed feelings about the DOC's reentry plan. They see it as limited, something that stops at the gate. Plus, they say, prison reentry coordinators often have to wear a number of hats, and don't have time to spend on in-depth planning for soon-to-be-released inmates.

Nevertheless, with a top-level administrator's enthusiasm for statistics, Craig is bullish on Iowa's recidivism rate, which in 2016 hovers at 29 percent. Compare this to the national average of 50 percent. The state also recently received a big recidivism reduction grant. The goal is to get it down to 20-22 percent. That would be huge.[38]

Of course, statistics like these don't always paint the full picture. And reducing recidivism isn't the only way to measure success. We don't really follow up on whether those who are released lead productive, healthy, fulfilling lives.

Craig believes one way to reduce the prison population is by putting more resources into community corrections, the system of parole and probation that allows offenders to return to society, under supervision. Communication between parole counselors, parole officers on the street and parolees is particularly important. (Prison Policy Initiative actually gives failing grades to a majority of states, including Iowa, for having few elements of a fair and equitable parole system.)[39]

And although he doesn't say as much, I sense that Craig would love to see more funding put into the Department of Corrections, to offer more and better programming.

Which, of course, depends on legislative priorities, and also, on how we all think about prisons.

One of the hardest things about life inside, Patrick had decided, was the close proximity to other people, many of whom he would prefer not to be around at all. He couldn't escape the feeling that they were all living in a kind of shadowland, that those around him were just passing time in a gloomy holding pattern. Such a perspective allowed people to escape into fantasy and isolation.

He did have moments of illumination. He had received a letter from his stepdaughter after her first week in college. She was doing well, had a good roommate, and was happy. And she missed him. She was his sweetheart, the last child he would ever raise. She was not much of a child anymore, of course, but she still acted like his kid.

Although his stepdaughter had been writing regularly, he'd heard nothing from his wife for almost four months. No mail, no visits, no email, no money. She hadn't answered any of his letters. Patrick was worried, but there was nothing he could do but wait.

He complained, when he could, about the phone service. In his opinion, it was a racket. The company providing it focused only on prison phone service, and their profits were enormous. County jail had been the worst; his wife had paid $29 to receive a 15-minute call from him.

Patrick stretched his legs, folding his arms behind his head. From time to time he allowed himself to indulge in thinking about his early life. Childhood memories drifted into the light of awareness: he remembered bats winging across the summer Baltimore night sky; excavating in the backyard for his rock collection; and he thought of his pet rabbit, Hopsie. At six—was he six?—he and his parents had traveled to the World's Fair in New York, where he remembered hearing the song, "It's a Small World After All."

In fourth grade he'd begun singing at Old St. Paul's Cathedral in downtown Baltimore and was selected for the part of Amahl in "Amahl and the Night Visitors." This was when singing first really captivated him. It was at the cast party, though, that he heard a different kind of music—Led Zeppelin's "Whole Lotta Love." It blew him away.

It was also around this time that he tried his first cigarette. That nasty habit, he reflected, would continue for forty years.

He'd been a smart kid, consistently testing in the top one percent of his school. But though he would have loved to participate in sports, he was a slow runner due to an orthopedic problem, and this left him feeling left out. Academics didn't matter much to him, and in fact, he found that getting good grades made him unpopular.

A howl echoed from somewhere down the unit. Patrick looked up, then returned to his reverie.

It was the 'bad boys,' he'd noticed, who achieved notoriety, which he mistook for popularity. He started emulating them and won a few admirers. Seventh grade turned out to be like gladiator school. He ended up in the principal's office at least once a week for fighting, and got ejected from the classroom regularly for taking on the mantle of class clown.

Things weren't going so well at home, either. His parents cut corners on his wardrobe, buying his clothes off clearance racks. This, he felt, set him apart from other kids.

Why had his folks been so damned strict? His bedtime had remained at 7:30 p.m. until he was almost fifteen. On summer evenings he heard the shouts and laughter of kids streaming through his bedroom window, long after he was in bed. Other kids got to go more places and do more things than he did, and he resented it. He had lain awake and dreamed of being free.

What about that girl? Libby, a red-haired minister's daughter. He'd fallen for her, hard. Unfortunately, she hadn't returned his affections.

Patrick rolled over on his bunk and sighed.

On his thirteenth birthday things had come to a head. The day hadn't started well. He accidentally broke a window in the garage, and his parents grounded him. Libby came by for a short time, but she seemed indifferent to him. She finally told him she was going out with someone else. Patrick was devastated. He pushed out the front door past his folks, declaring that he was leaving home and blaming them for his misery. Then he ran.

A neighbor discovered Patrick crouching behind some bushes and persuaded him to return home and tough it out. His parents were impatient as he continued to rant about his life and how they were ruining it. They eventually pinned him to the floor in the entrance hall, and scrubbed his face vigorously with a wet washcloth, trying to bring him down from "the LSD trip" they thought he was on.

The irony was, he wouldn't start using drugs until he was fifteen.

NINE

Call Me By My Name

STAND UP, SIT DOWN, stand up. In rehearsal we're constantly standing to sing and then sitting back down to look through our folders for the next piece. The man sitting next to me musters himself each time and stands with a groan. After we finish a song Mary says, "You can sit," and he lowers himself with a sigh. *Can't we just sit the whole time?*

Some guys perch on the edge of their seats, their spinal columns aligned with greater purpose. A couple of men slump, subverting the norm, refusing to stand while the rest of us practice a song. Maybe they slouch because that's the only position their bodies can manage in the moment.

But standing, showing up, having a good attitude, is something the choir aims to encourage. On the other side of me is an upbeat man named Brett. He's been working in the psych unit; his positive attitude is infectious. "These guys spend all day in their rooms. So when they go out, I go in, sweep, mop, change the sheets. I think they really appreciate it." He smiles.

I double-check his nametag. Even though I've seen many of these guys for a number of rehearsals, their names don't always sink in.

"I'm terrible with names, too," he says.

For most of the day, people in prison are addressed (or admonished) by their last names by prison staff. It reminds me a little of P.E. class back in the day, when coaches would harangue us, using our last names, if we didn't shimmy up a rope fast enough.

Many inmates call each other by their last names, too, I've noticed. Perhaps this is a way to avoid appearing too vulnerable. In the choir, we use first names, which creates a sense of familiarity and belonging. As a way to get to know each other, we often go around the circle before rehearsal and speak our names.

Because really, who doesn't want to be called by their name, seen and known? Who doesn't want to be remembered in this way?

An insider named Chip shares a memory with me. It's cool in the gymnasium where we're standing. (We sometimes rehearse in the gym to prepare for our concerts). He tells me he likes it that way. "I grew up in a house without heating. My mother used to heat bricks and put them in our beds to keep our feet warm."

It's a simple image, tethering Chip to his childhood, a lifeline to an age of innocence.

How does prison shape the fickle connect-the-dots mechanism of memory? Is memory sharpened by longing? Dulled by attrition? Is it a refuge to be clung to like a drowning man to a rock?

As the men sit in their cells, some may drift back to the taste of their mother's casseroles, or the aroma of coffee and sweet rolls wafting from the kitchen on a wintry morning. They may recall the front porch of their homes where they listened to music, or flash on an image of backyard barbecue, smoke and horseshoes.

One man remembers standing tall on the green grass, under the blue sky, in center field, waiting for a ball to drop into his glove.

Keith, longing for summer nights of freedom, sprawls in his memory on the hood of his car, surrounded by friends, a guitar within grasp, looking up at the sky, at the stars. After all this time inside, he thinks, do those stars remember my name?

Henry says, "A man told me it had been three years since he'd had any orange juice. Seems a little careless of one's wellbeing to keep track of things like that. I enjoy hearing about the pleasures and privileges the world affords. But it seems morbid to measure their exact distance from me. If I know the world I left still lives and its pleasures persist, then I can easily imagine that I will someday return to them."

Like the singing of "Sittin' on the Dock of the Bay", certain activities bring pleasurable memories, reminding insiders that the world has not entirely forgotten them, if only because they have not forgotten the world.

One young man tells me he was born and raised twenty miles from the prison. He has fond memories of the work he did on his family's farm there. *We had cows, chickens, pigs, mostly dairy. I loved milking those cows, taking care of them. The reason I loved it was because I was providing milk to people, and nourishment. That was the important thing. I used to be on the tractor until 10, 11 at night. I just liked it.*

But when they return to their cells at night, some of these men are also haunted by memories of their crimes, which replay over and over again in their minds.

The moment dark anger roils over, the gun goes off, fist crunches bone.

The moment of pocketing the cash, violating the boundary, breaking the trust.

The moment of betrayal.

⸙

Choral director Robert Shaw writes that choral music and other arts have as their concern "the intellectual, ethical and spiritual maturity of human life." [40] That sounds about right. In the choir, when we relax into a sense of being who we're supposed to be, such maturity can be freeing. When we come together, paying close attention, singing from the heart, it *is* a liberating thing.

Perhaps intellectual, ethical and spiritual maturity should be the goal of criminal justice as well. Our society seems to struggle to muster the "right" response to crime. What does justice look like? Should our collective motivation be based in revenge or rehabilitation? We've learned, mostly, that revenge doesn't make things right. But when the bonds of civil connection are broken, how do we make them whole again? How truly concerned are we with the wholeness of men and women in prison?

In this time and place, sending people to prison is the de facto punishment for crime, something we accept without much thought. But I've discovered that incarceration as a primary punishment in the West really only dates to the early 19th century.

Punishment has taken many forms throughout human history. Binding to a stake, ritual cursing, stoning, barred social interaction—that's what pre-Common Era justice looked like in some parts of the world. Old Testament justice, epitomized by the idea of 'an eye for an eye', was designed to maintain tribal unity, a step in the development of social systems—the establishment of a body of justice whose purpose was to enact the retaliation and claim exclusive right to punish.

Sub-Saharan Africa dealt with those who broke the social code through beatings, banishment, or poison, but the focus was on victim compensation, especially through restoration of property. China, until the third century, employed beatings and executions.

In England, confinement in workhouses did exist as early as the 17th century, as a cure for the 'idleness' of the poor. But banishment, whipping, hanging, and fines were more common and these carried over into early American justice.

Like Australia, the United States was colonized in part by those who had transgressed, and in part by those who pretended never to transgress. The British parliament shipped more than 30,000 convicts to the new world between 1718 and 1775.

Colonial America was composed of small, tight communities, built around ideas about God, punishment and the social order, under obedience to a hierarchy of fathers and ministers, Lawrence Friedman writes.[41] Punishment often consisted of public shaming, like putting people in stocks. Scarlet letters, famously, were sewn onto clothing for some offenses. Crimes against morality, including the crime of missing church, could get you punished. The poor and slaves were whipped regularly; the wealthy, rarely.

But a society short on labor was reluctant to put people away and the practice of incarceration was still rare.

With the American Revolution came reform. The Bill of Rights codified ideas about fair trials. "English criminal justice was a patriarchal jumble, a peculiar mix of extreme legalism and extreme discretion," Friedman writes. "In a republican criminal justice system, all crimes and their punishments would be embodied in a clear definitive code." Reformers began to push for prisons as an enlightened alternative to earlier harsh punishments.

As our country entered the 19th century, two competing visions of incarceration held sway. One, centered in Pennsylvania, encouraged the isolation of prisoners in small cells, clothed in scratchy uniforms, alone and with no distractions, so that they could meditate on their sins and become penitent (from whence the word 'penitentiary.') Based on the ideas of reformer Benjamin Rush, who saw the need for 'houses of repentance,' this vision was grounded in a Christian, especially Quaker, worldview.

Unfortunately, the isolation drove people crazy. Charles Dickens visited some of these prisons and said the prisoners were "dead to everything but torturing anxieties and horrible despair."

"I hold this slow and daily tampering with the mysteries of the brain," Dickens wrote, "to be immeasurably worse than any torture of the body: and because its ghastly signs and tokens are not so palpable to the eye and sense of touch as scars upon the flesh; because its wounds are not upon the surface, and it extorts few cries that human ears can hear; therefore I the more denounce it, as a secret punishment which slumbering humanity is not roused up to stay."[42]

In contrast to this was the congregate system, developed in Auburn, N.Y., where inmates could mingle while at hard labor, though there was enforced silence at all times and they were separated into small cells at night. This system seemed to win out in the debate over the future of the U.S. penal system and gave birth to America's first maximum-security prison, Sing Sing, located on the Hudson River, coining the phrase "going up the river." Iowa adopted the Auburn system in 1839 when it built its first penitentiary at Fort Madison.

By the time of the Civil War, the congregate system was in place throughout the North and Midwest. The prevailing notion was that people turned to crime because of defective background, weak wills, and bad company. Prison addressed these problems by providing "backbone."

But maintaining even the congregate system was expensive; it was cheaper to let prisons get noisy and crowded. And states couldn't resist making money off of prisoners by leasing them out to local manufacturers and farmers. This practice raised protests from unions, who saw prison's cheap labor as a threat to the power of organized labor.

Reformers organized a national congress on reformatory discipline in 1870, ushering in the "second great penal movement." Wielding a declaration of principles, an emphasis on professional guard training, religious instruction, and moral regeneration, the movement focused on reforming inmates' characters.

The river of incarceration in our country also has a muddier tributary: prison system as slave plantation. Though some states in the south used penitentiaries, many, like South Carolina, the most conservative state in the slave belt, never did. Chain gangs were more common there and convicts were sent out to work for plantations.

According to historian Robert Perkinson, "Two ancestral lines come into view: one reformatory, one retributive; one integrative, one exclusionary; one conceived in northern churches and the other on southern work farms…"[43]

"The Southern argument is that prisons today operate in a retributive mode that has long been practiced and promoted in the South," Perkinson continues. There are, for example, still a number of prison farms on the grounds of old plantations, such as Angola Prison in Louisiana. Such prisons, he writes, hold a racial charge, with white supremacy as their real aim. The idea of revenge, not rehabilitation or restoration, as the main focus, seems to be deeply rooted in many of these Southern prisons, even today.

One of the biggest tools the DOC uses to force compliance and punish offenders is to take away your identity as a person. On the street, I was many things: a biker, a drug dealer, a leader, a friend, a parent, a consumer, etc. I was a multifaceted individual with certain tastes and the right and ability to indulge them. In prison, I was an offender, #1092777, society's outcast. I had no personal identity.

— Patrick

TEN

Keith Loses Control

CHOIR VOLUNTEERS DON'T USUALLY know the crimes of which inside singers have been convicted. I think most of us take pains not to research those details, though they're a matter of public record. Sure, we may be curious. But we don't need to know, and leaving it a mystery levels the playing field. It means that no matter what someone has done, their place in this community is assured.

However, in order to appreciate and learn from the arc of a full story, from offense to punishment to post-release, it's useful to know the details of at least one person's crime. Keith filled me in on his.

In the diffuse gloom of the late hours one night in early December 2007, while driving aimlessly around the countryside outside a small central Iowa city, Keith lost control. High on meth, skidding off the road, his car landed in a ditch and got stuck in the mud and snow.

His cell phone was dead. In no state of mind to clearly consider his options, he did what he was accustomed to doing. He sat behind the wheel, the cold wind blowing across the fields buffeting his car, and smoked more meth.

After a while, though he doesn't remember making the decision to do so, he got out of his car and walked to a nearby farmhouse. A porch light was on. He knocked, but no one answered. Walking around to the back of the house, he noticed an open back porch door. Shivering with cold, he entered the house.

What happened next is a bit of a blur, but he remembers being confronted by the owner of the house, an older man, and getting into some kind of fight with him. Keith is tall and muscular. The two scuffled, knocking over some furniture, and at one point he looped a cord around the man's neck. Realizing the rashness of this act, and knowing that he had to get out of there, Keith left the house and sprinted to his car. His brain was reeling.

A passing driver stopped to offer assistance. The man helped pull his car out, and Keith sped off. Still in a fog, he tossed out the rest of his drugs and made his way home. For a full day and night he sat in his apartment, paralyzed by paranoia. What exactly had happened? Was the old man all right?

He can't recall everything that occurred during those few days. He doesn't really remember thinking at all.

In the end, he went to the police station, still under the influence of all the meth he'd smoked, and turned himself in.

In court, the prosecuting attorney wanted to throw the book at him. He was charged with a number of offenses, including 1st degree burglary, attempted murder, and willful injury. Keith was advised to plead guilty to 1st degree burglary. He used an 'Alford Plea,' a guilty plea without direct admission of guilt, which allowed him to receive less time.

Members of his family sat, stricken, in the courtroom, watching the proceedings. They were having a hard time wrapping their minds around what had happened. Though they were supportive, they made it clear that they were disappointed. As he sat there waiting to receive his sentence, he felt as low as he'd ever had in his life. He was 26 years old. He would spend nearly the next seven years inside.

To family and friends, Keith had always been the guy who led a normal, even enviable, life: he was married and had a full-time job.

But he himself suspected he was on a path to an early death—nights of drinking and drugs so intense they were lost to his memory, his arms marked with purple scars from an endless series of needles. His eyes in those days were sunken into his face, his skin hung on a bony frame. Any money he earned or stole he spent on alcohol and drugs rather than on food.

Keith's letters to me expressed a clear-eyed acknowledgment of his situation and a commitment to try to change. As I opened and read them, I began to get a sense of his approach to life.

He says he was raised to respect himself and others. "I was brought up with the standard Midwestern values, the Golden Rule and what have you. I just had a desire for drugs that overshadowed those. At times I hated myself."

"Most of my life was spent standing at a crossroads, between two paths. I took one path finally. Now I'm just trying to make a better path."

Sometimes I envision the men lying on their bunks at night, their arms tucked behind their heads, gripped by the ghostly companionship of their own stories, wondering how to turn those stories into songs. Slowly they roll over and scribble a few, preliminary lines, experimenting with rhyme schemes. Some are beginning to recognize the rhythmic and melodic hooks that catch a listener's attention, as songwriters from Tin Pan Alley to Motown have done for decades.

Like a successful TV series, the Oakdale Community Choir has generated spinoffs. As it became clear that insiders had a lot to say, and the talent to express it, a Songwriting Workshop was born.

Every Tuesday afternoon, an hour before the choir convenes as a whole, guys file into the testing room, take their seats and begin warming up. Mary Cohen leads the group in melodic improvisation. They sit forward in their seats, concentrating. Sing a note and try to match your neighbor. Now, match this beat, beat it out against your thigh. The men follow along, clapping what is at first a simple rhythmic pattern, but which eventually becomes more complicated. (These exercises often find their way into choir practice, too.)

They work from sight-reading books for a while, trying to master simple tunes by seeing them on the page. After this they divide into smaller groups to work on developing their own lyrics and melodies. Mary is there to help, as is music student Rose, accompanist Colin, and Catherine Wilson.

Wilson has been working on her own PhD dissertation, about songwriting in prisons. She suggests that it's a remarkable thing when you can create a safe space inside, as is done in the workshop.[44] Writing songs offers one way to express deeply felt and difficult emotions. The tough-guy exterior can be laid aside for the moment.

The questions about identity raised in a previous chapter take on added significance here. Besides learning musical skills, the participants have an opportunity to reflect on things like self-control and maturity. If one aspect of being a man means taking more responsibility for one's actions and being less selfish, then participation in the choir and the workshop offers a bit of space to grow into these qualities.

Repressed feelings bubble up: Regret. Shame. Perplexity. Grief for their actions, and awareness of the grief of their victims. They may feel they're beginning to come to terms with what they've done, to crack the carapace of unexpressed emotion and experience that was long considered too painful to let out. You can sense this in a song like "Missing for So Long".

Jeremy wrote the song for his two young sons, expressing his anguish at not being there for them. He hopes he can get to know them, someday, though he won't be free until his boys are grown men.

"You reached for my hand, it wasn't there. It's been missing for years. One day it was there to help soothe away your fears, the next it wasn't and I let you fall. And I'm sorry that . . .

My guiding hand can't help you along, it's been bound and hidden, missing for so long. Gone and not there, you need to be strong, to not lose hope, and hope it's not long."

Knowing that their partners have been forced to raise children alone, to keep a family together while they're inside, some of the men are hit hard by these lyrics. "Daddy is in prison" is a trope that elicits tears.

The song "Mary, Mary" is a gift from one of the insiders to his wife, written with help from several workshop members. The couple married in 2010, while the man was in prison, and he promised to remarry her upon his release.

My heart is in your hands. I'm not trying to possess you, or making rash demands. I'm just longing for a future with the only girl who understands, and I find your love extraordinary, Mary.

Another song birthed in workshop, "Tapestry", reflects on the cumulative nature of time:

Day after day we keep weaving the tapestry of our lives, assisted by our children, our good friends, our lovers, or wives,

Created from the threads of the moments that make up our days, gathered from the highways and the byways, and the lesser-known ways.

As the men begin to feel more at ease, a sense of fun takes over, reflected in this parody of *West Side Story's* "Dear Officer Krupke."

"Dear Warden Craig-ee, you gotta understand. We're stuck here in prison, which puts us in your hand.

Our mothers are heartbroken, our fathers really care. Golly Moses, naturally we're scared!"

Some of the men come into the workshop already possessing chops in terms of being able to sing, read, and write music. Others haven't a clue.

But most learn enough over time to be able to get their musical thoughts down on paper.

These might be just a few words on a page with lines indicating a basic melodic contour. But proto-songs soon become more complex, with pitches and rhythms notated on staff paper. It's the first step in the process of fleshing out, revising, sharing, and eventually performing their songs.

Once they have a rough draft, they bring the song to Workshop. A man reads the lyrics or performs his song in front of the group, sometimes with help from others, but more often alone. Then he receives feedback, with a facilitator reminding everyone to focus on the song's strengths. Such feedback is, as anyone who's done creative work knows, very helpful, both in terms of reflecting an objective view of the work, and in building the writer's confidence. Imagine the satisfaction an insider must feel at having one of their songs birthed into the world in this way.

Laresse Harvey, a former inmate cited in both Wilson's and Cohen's research, says that, "a reintegration process that includes writing, poetry, music and drama could help to reduce recidivism and produce productive citizens."[45]

Speaking from experience, Harvey says, "I'm a part of what the arts can offer. Hope...change...second chances."

A warden at the Chino State Prison in California describes how music contributes to inmates' opportunities to build self-respect. He notes what should be obvious: "Prisoners have the same emotions and ambitions as other human beings. The mere fact that they are incarcerated does not stamp out those desires and ambitions."

I love the colorful account about the creative work of one band conductor, relayed by warden Clinton T. Duffy, of the San Quentin prison, back in 1955. [46]He described the impact of a dance band led by John Kendricks, former army bandmaster who was serving a life sentence:

"John coaxed, threatened, and cussed those musicians at rehearsals far into the night, a prison Toscanini who was determined to show that murderers, thugs, and thieves can also have music in their hearts and perhaps play as well as most orchestras outside. I could hardly believe my eyes sometimes, watching certain gangsters and tough guys meekly taking John's caustic rebukes, but they had respect for his musicianship and were anxious to please. John's first jazz concert in the mess hall nearly shook the girders out of the roof, and a stranger might have thought it was a riot. The waiters took up the beat with their big metal spoons, plates were banged on the table tops and men stomped their feet on the concrete floor."

"There was such an upsurge in morale inside those ancient walls after the first few concerts that I decided to have the orchestra at the noon meal more often, and sometimes there was an extra performance at night which went into the cells via the newly installed prison radio network. All the inmates were proud of their hardworking band, and that pride was shown in their conduct and their work. Before long, various carefully selected lodges, clubs and groups of peace officers from nearby towns were invited to hear the band, and word soon spread around about the new spirit in the big house by the bay."

Such programs continued on through the last half of the 20th century. M. Elsila describes teaching a music theory and songwriting class in two Michigan prisons. He used a "liberatory musicology" methodology and collaborated with students on larger, activist issues through music with the hope of working toward positive social change. [47]

Teamwork, group order, social adjustment, new companionship, fair play and sense of cooperation, decreased prejudice and a healthy sense of community cohesiveness, all of these qualities have been noted in studies of music's effect on insiders.

So why, in recent years, has funding for the arts and music in prisons been cut? Many correctional facilities these days lack any programs that allow for individual expression. Some arts programs still exist, but they're far fewer in number compared to the extent of programming and organized support that existed in 1980.

For example, the Arts-in-Corrections program in California lost its funding in 2003, and in 2010 all artist facilitator positions were eliminated. This, despite a 1983 study indicating that AIC was cost-effective. (The program was partially restored in 2014). [48]

In many American prisons, writing and other remedial programs have been or are being cut back substantially. "I believe we began to incarcerate more people than the system could handle, and all treatment programs suffered with the buildup of what has been termed the prison industrial complex," arts consultant Grady Hillman writes. "Suddenly prisons were all about bed space...as a financial resource and locating prisoners as a commodity market." [49]

Also, "Many arts-in-corrections programs were running away from exposure," Hillman continues, "fearful that the public would decry such programs as contributing to the common clichéd perception that we were somehow running country clubs."

"Prison systems were hearing from the public and politicians that we needed to hurt inmates, not help them."

⚜

And out of what one sees and hears and out of what one feels, Wallace Stevens wrote, *who could've thought to make so many selves, so many sensuous worlds?*

One day, a few outsiders get the chance to taste the fruits of all this songwriting labor. Those of us able to attend the midday concert are ushered into the testing room. I exchange nods with a couple of the guys who are sitting at the front of the room.

The show kicks off with "Dance of Life", a tango inspired, says the composer Chester, by a scene in the film *True Lies*. Chester is a jovial middle-aged African-American; I always enjoy interacting with him.

"Hello there, young man," he'll say to me in rehearsal. "Where've you been?"

"Oh, here and there."

"And everywhere?"

His song is not the usual choir fare. It's catchy and complex, with lyrics full of longing and romance:

I feel a gentle breeze, its fingers caressing my face. A toast to destiny, my future is walking this way. I've seen this face before, but only in my dreams. It's meant to be, just you and me, in the dance of life.

Moved and surprised, we applaud. This song is definitely going to spice up our concert repertoire. Terence is up next. A tall, thin, bespectacled man, he's penned an overtly religious song—"Mourning is Broken"—taking the traditional (and Cat Stevens-popularized) song, and bringing new lyrics to it, suggesting the end of despair that can be found in religious experience. It's also a beautiful song.

Darrell is a young white man I've watched gesticulate with his hands to the beat when he sings. He and outsider Jen perform a song they've worked on together, Darrell cautiously strumming the guitar. Though this song seems undeveloped, in a few years I'll hear Darrell perform the solo to another song he's written, a beautiful tune that he sings with confidence and flair, and I'll think, "How this guy has grown."

Finally, an older white man stands before the group. He smiles.

"You can call me Bio Bill. That's what I've got nicknamed, 'cause of my job. I work in security, and I kind of wear three hats in security. I'm a janitor, I'm a runner, which goes down to the units and gets the guys and brings them back down to the units and back and forth, acting like an escort. And the third thing is, one hour a day, I pick up biohazards on all the units. I hit all of the units in about an hour, and seven days a week I do that. So this is my little Bio Bill Blues."

As the accompanist picks out the introduction on guitar, the songwriter pulls on a pair of gloves and a biohazard mask, just as he would if he were preparing for work. He holds his hands in front of him at face level as a surgeon might before an operation. The audience is delighted by this gesture. Then he pulls down his mask and begins to sing.

We go out a rollin' right after noon count, I said we go out a rollin' right after noon count. Go to my closet, get that red cart out.
My red cart and me, we go out every day. I said my red cart and me, we go out every day. We travel the halls, keeping Oakdale safe.
You see them old germs, don't like me at all. I said you see them old germs, don't like me at all. Puttin' on the gloves, they begin to fall.
Now, you've heard my story, I swear it's true. I said now you've heard my story, I swear it's true. My name is Bio Bill, and I'm a member of the GP Crew!

ELEVEN

Another Day in Paradise

As if trying to fill a void, Patrick tried everything in his teen years: pot, hash, Valium, Librium, LSD, cocaine, psilocybin mushrooms, peyote, mescaline, Quaaludes, and other assorted pills and powders. The only drugs he didn't try were opium, heroin, and morphine.

His favorites were marijuana and the hallucinogens. By 16, he was selling pot and acid to schoolmates and friends. Most of the money he earned went to pay for his own personal supply. He was busted twice in high school by school authorities, once for possession of pot and a pipe, and once for selling a gram of hash to a school informant.

Another incident was a little more serious. He had given a neighbor $50 to buy a quarter pound of Mexican weed. The boy kept the money, didn't produce the weed, and started to avoid him. Patrick told a friend from school about it, and the friend loaned him his father's Colt .45. Patrick hid it under his mattress and phoned the kid. He was gonna shoot him if he didn't give the money back, he warned. The boy's father was listening in on an extension and promptly called the cops.

The police arrived at Patrick's house, searched his bedroom, and found the gun. He was charged with assault by threatening, but the charge was dropped because he was a juvenile from a good home. But it was still his first charge; like most of the ones to follow, it involved drugs and guns.

His dealing would continue for the next thirty-three years, off and on. Mostly on. Even when working legal jobs, Patrick continued to sell drugs on the side. He sold full-time for sixteen of those years, his only source of income.

One looks for reasons a person goes down this path. Were there hereditary factors at play, his biological parents providing influential genes? (Patrick had been adopted, and didn't know his birth parents). Was it the effect of bullying? Bad company? Were his parents too strict? It's not easy to say. I know from my own early life that when you feel left out, drugs and alcohol can be plenty attractive.

There were some promising moments. Patrick moved from Maryland to Iowa to attend Simpson College, a good school. But in 1976 the drug market was in high gear. His drug use at college became so bad that he eventually had to drop out. He didn't tell his parents where he was going, just quit and moved to Ottumwa to live with a girl he'd met at a party. She was nineteen, with a six-month old baby. Patrick was still seventeen.

He figured he could make enough money dealing so that he wouldn't have to work, but it was slow going in the beginning. There were plenty of other dealers in the area, including a group of outlaw bikers. Patrick was impressed with their swagger, and he envied their lifestyle. He started hanging out with a group called the Grim Reapers.

Then he got busted for possession for the first time and went to jail. He sat inside for two weeks. The charges were dismissed because the arresting officer hadn't had a search warrant.

After this he began dealing methamphetamines on a large scale. He soon learned how to make his own. The shape of those days is a blur to him now: running with bikers, collecting knives, handguns, and assault rifles and making lots of money. He was also sleeping only one night out of every two weeks.

You could say he was living life completely outside the law.

You could also say he was on the radar of Southeast Iowa law enforcement.

Not long after, the Des Moines police arrested him and charged him with numerous drug offenses. He was convicted, sentenced to 25 years, and he entered prison for the first time.

In the 1936 MGM comic short film, "How to be a Detective," actor Robert Benchley swivels expertly to the camera and begins to expound on 'criminal types.' There are, he says, certain typical physical features by which you can identify a criminal, such as a sloping forehead, or a weak chin. As he describes these qualities, he asks a sketch artist to create a composite drawing of a criminal with these various traits.

The joke, of course, is that the resulting picture looks just like him.

(It *is* a joke. Clearly, neither physiognomy nor ethnicity is a predictor of criminal behavior.)

There's a long history of using humor to navigate the painful topic of crime and criminals, from the jocular phrases inmates use to describe their home (the big house, the joint, the slammer) to gallows humor. Humor helps a person to cope, and in prison, this is especially important. It becomes a normalizing force, wiping away distinctions, releasing tensions.

Quick! Where's the best place to start a prison choir? Sing Sing, of course.

A lot of men in the choir are able to crack me up. For example, there's Anthony, a burly Latino 20-something, who possesses an extraordinary voice—a pure, high tenor. I learn from one of the other insiders that he has aspirations to become an opera singer, though he's never mentioned it himself. He's also a very funny guy.

"How's it going?" I ask him one afternoon.

"Oh, you know, just another day in paradise."

While we're practicing the traditional American ballad "Shenandoah," which contains the line, "Oh, Shenandoah, I love your daughter," a Correctional Officer pokes his head into the room. He's obviously someone with whom Anthony has a joking relationship, though what Anthony does next strikes me as particularly ballsy.

He sings out, "Oh, Officer Smith, I love your daughter…" and the room explodes in laughter.

Paul, whom I stand next to for much of my second season, is a short white man with longish hair, a potbelly, and a quip for any occasion. As he walks among the rows with a stack of new songs, handing out scores, he'll joke, "It's hard to get good help nowadays."

To a flautist rehearsing with the choir for a special piece, a prim-looking woman, he calls out, "Dude, play some Tull!"

And when Mary reminds the choir of the importance of showing up to every rehearsal, of commitment, Paul pipes up, "No problem. I've already been committed."

An inside joke, I guess.

Sometimes I'm stymied by remarks that seem to spring from a lack of self-esteem. As I take a seat in the back row, Jack, a young white man turns and says half-jokingly, "Hey, you're sitting back here with the ugly people." I smile, a little uncomfortably.

At the end of rehearsal, the group assembles itself into a circle, and I find myself peering around the room at these people and thinking about their stories. This circle, in its equality of participation—no one above or below anyone else, no one barking out or responding to orders—offers a sense of belonging that seems rare.

Mary prompts us with one of her exercises: Say two or three words that describe how you're feeling about the choir right now.

"Peace and joy," someone pipes up.

"Music and community."

"Music lifts up."

And then, from one new insider, "Slightly confused."

There's more laughter.

Beneath a chair in the tenor section sprawls a puppy, a Yellow Lab of infinite cuteness. It scratches its ear with a long hind leg, looking expectantly to its human for a treat.

Its human is one of several inside choir members who have been selected to become dog trainers—a new program in the prison—and they've begun bringing their "wards" with them to rehearsal. If you've ever looked into the bright eyes of a Labrador, you'll understand the appeal. Spending time with animals helps socialize people. Staff members stop to pet the dog, they talk with the inmate, and connections spring up between everybody. Caring for these animals, insiders develop a sense of responsibility.

A dog person myself, I find myself hovering over the pups, lavishing them with affection, and asking for details on their progress. One song we're working on features whistling passages, and as sixty sets of lips purse in high-pitched trills, you can imagine what happens next. Furry ears perk; sometimes the dogs join in.

Oakdale is affiliating with a group called Retrieving America, allowing these trained puppies to be given as service animals to veterans with PTSD. The dogs are also used for therapy here in the forensic hospital, especially with mentally ill inmates. And there's interest in training dogs to work with autistic kids.

The program is the brainchild of current warden James McKinney, who has come on board after the promotion of Daniel Craig. Everyone I speak with—inside or out—says McKinney is a remarkably benevolent prison official. In line with his radical philosophy of treating inmates like human beings, he's materialized a number of new ideas.

The florescent lights are off in McKinney's office as we talk, and soft light seeps in from the windows overlooking the parking lot.

"I tell the guys, 'You've taken something from someone else, caused tears and pain,'" McKinney says. "Now when you give that dog away, you're experiencing loss, too, like your victims did. But this time it's going to be for good instead of evil."

A nontraditional kind of warden, he sees programs like the choir as a way to create connections. "You find as many ways as you can to build a connection," he says about his approach. "You open things up. Offer group activities. I never limit the possibilities. I can't pick and choose what activities there are—that might benefit only a few people."

"We have to believe in these folks," he goes on. "We have to give them not only second chances, but third, fourth, fifth and sixth chances. They have to know that someone is in their corner."

It wasn't always this way for McKinney.

When he first got into corrections, it was just a job. Frankly, he says, he saw inmates as commodities. He was working at a jail, not a prison, and saw the worst side of people—those who were intoxicated, had beaten someone, or were in for murder. He treated them with basic respect, as he was required to do, but otherwise never gave them much thought.

Then an 18-year old kid came in on a minor charge. McKinney began talking with the kid, asked him why he was getting into trouble. The boy said it was because of where he lived, his environment growing up. Was this a good excuse? McKinney points out that he himself had also grown up in difficult circumstances, but had turned out OK.

The kid was released, but within two weeks was back in jail for slitting the throat of a salesman. He would spend the rest of his life in prison.

"And I asked myself, was it just him? Or did we do something wrong?"

This was the beginning of a process of reflection for McKinney. How do you treat people when they're in prison, he wondered, how can you have an impact on them, so that they don't come back once they're released?

McKinney now believes rehabilitation begins when you get inmates to start to see past themselves. Programs like dog training or the choir help them learn how to give back, instead of just taking all the time. Shifting the focus off of themselves, they begin to develop empathy. And empathy is at the heart of rehabilitation. It's a conviction McKinney will emphasize repeatedly when he speaks to the audience at our choir concerts, especially the inmate portion of the audience: Become responsible, become less selfish. That's what it's all about.

"It's not always easy," he emphasizes. "My approach can aggravate some of the staff. Most of them like the way I do business, though. The inmates do, too. I've had good success. Sometimes former inmates will call out to me when I'm out in public and say our place made a difference in their lives. It helped to get that one encouraging word from someone."

Perhaps, McKinney muses, working in a prison is a little like coaching. You encourage, you lead, you pat people on the back. You coax them to change, not by berating them, but by telling them how good they could be.

There's a question I've been wrestling with for a while, and I put it to him. Can everyone be rehabilitated?

McKinney pauses, and runs a hand through his graying hair.

"Everyone can get better. I'm not sure everyone can be fully rehabilitated, sadly. We treat everyone with respect, and we work our tails off. My favorite inmate has been in prison for 54 years. He's the nicest, most upbeat, gracious person. He teaches English to Spanish-speaking inmates. But he'll die in prison."

"Still, if I'd met him two days after he murdered someone, I'd have never thought he could change. Time does change things."

I want to ask McKinney what it means that someone who is upbeat and gracious, and has been in prison for more than 50 years, is not yet recognized as rehabilitated. This touches on broader questions, though, of sentencing reform, and how the system recognizes when a person has been legitimately reformed. These are not questions that a prison warden is tasked with answering.

But in terms of the direct prison experience, McKinney's ideas seem to be gaining traction. Part of the challenge is getting his staff on board. Do most COs embrace the philosophy of "engaging with and respecting prisoners?"

"They're getting a lot better at it," McKinney says. "Of course, if you're a CO in a unit with a hundred guys, and one guy is getting mad, and you tell him to go to his cell, and he refuses, and the other ninety-nine are watching, you're going to feel apprehension. The CO thinks he'll be safer with stricter controls."

Before they begin work, COs receive four weeks of training, in detail work, conducting pat searches, and on how to protect themselves. But 98 percent of prison work is about communication, McKinney says, and he would like to spend more time training COs to communicate well.

Violent incidents do happen occasionally, often due to mental health issues. There's less violence, however, and less gang behavior, at Oakdale than at other Iowa prisons.

Still, it can be a stressful place to work; there have been a few staff suicides. "That's heartbreaking," McKinney says. "If there's a negative atmosphere at work, people may go home and drink, there's lots of stress. We try to create a more normal-feeling workplace, where people can laugh, or pet a dog. Then they can go home and relax."

He encourages his COs to let things go. Never, he says, take things personally.

That night I dream about the choir. The dream is rife with a sense of menace, of male bravado oozing out from the edges of things, of people jostling and one-upping each other. When I awake I consider how maybe my subconscious has linked up all my previously negative associations about prison and spilled them out in narrative form.

In the dream, a young insider steals my address book. I see he's tucked it under his music folder and I try to get it back. He's not supposed to know who I am in this way, to know my friends, my family, my contacts. When I try to retrieve it, he laughs.

Suddenly, though, another man stands up. He's in some kind of full costume, and he begins to sing. And people stop messing around; they focus on this man. Everyone is suddenly into this beautiful performance. We all dig it. It's as if all that blustery male energy has been overturned, channelized, made productive, by the power of the song.

TWELVE

Art Does Weird Things

The arts are not a way to make a living. They are a very human way of making life more bearable. Practicing an art, no matter how well or badly, is a way to make your soul grow, for heaven's sake. Sing in the shower. Dance to the radio. Tell stories. Write a poem to a friend, even a lousy poem. Do it as well as you possibly can. You will get an enormous reward. You will have created something.

— *Kurt Vonnegut*

I'M SITTING IN A sunny Iowa City coffee shop one late autumn morning, waiting to meet long-time prison educator Rachel Marie-Crane Williams.

She's a few minutes late and while waiting I look out the window and watch the goings-on in the courtyard of an adjoining preschool center. Two little boys are working out who gets to drive a small fire truck. There are a few tense moments, some tears.

My interviewee rushes in from a full day of meetings—besides being a University of Iowa art professor, she has an appointment as head of the women's studies department. Her Southern manner as she introduces herself is charming (she's originally from North Carolina). As the interview begins, we chat, among other things, about the cognitive dissonance that can take place working with prisoners—you get to know someone inside, get to like them, and then—bam!—you learn what they did. It can take some time to wrap your head around.

But Marie-Crane Williams has had time to work through such issues. She's taught in prisons across the country for decades, and for the past 15 years, has led art, creative writing and reading programs in Iowa prisons, mostly for women. She has plenty to say about how the arts contribute to rehabilitation.

"Art does weird things, unexpected things," she says. "It gives you a different way to think about identity. Prisoners can say to people 'I'm an artist,' and that explains a lot."

"So art is really useful. It gives people confidence. You can see improvement, growing self-esteem. The art class is a very unstructured space—they're free to talk and be normal. It's really helpful, just being in those spaces."

Art can also be a gateway to other educational experiences. Many prisoners have been traumatized by the mainstream educational system. They've been pushed out of it, and told they're failures. They may have lived an unstable life, in which education was not a consistent possibility. "Some have had 15 to 20 foster care placements, and that means 15 to 20 schools within four or five years."

Marie-Crane Williams appreciates the work the Oakdale choir is doing, because singing in prison can be a powerful thing. "Nobody sings there; they'll tell you to shut up. Personal space boundaries are intense. People don't want to listen. So singing is an act of resistance."

She recalls being at a prison workshop where, almost without reflecting on the significance of it, she was inspired to lead the inmates in a 'freedom song.' They started really getting into it, singing with conviction. And the officers became uneasy and came in to stop it. In prison, the evocation of freedom can be a fraught thing.

Art is also a huge part of the underground economy inside, from hand-drawn cards inmates send to their families to portraits. 'Draw me and my boyfriend together, that'll cost you 18 packs of ramen noodles.' Tattoos, which help to mark time, and to ritualize events, are also part of that economy. As are knitting and, yes, cheese making (straining the milk through socks). A whole economy thrives inside allowing people to create and exchange things.

"Everyone's struggling to make a mark on the world, to not be forgotten," Marie-Crane Williams says. "And art helps to ritualize our lives."

Marie-Crane Williams' work with women is something I'd like to learn more about. There are 832 percent more women in prison today than there were in 1977. Of course, there's been a 500 percent increase in incarceration overall since then. But the increase is higher for females.

"Women in prison have some issues that are similar to men's," she tells me, "but they also have different ones. They have higher rates of being sexually abused. They have more mental health concerns. They often lose their kids when they go inside. They may be dealing with poverty. They have chronic health issues, and substance abuse issues. They're often in destructive relationships, and when they get out, they still have to deal with those relationships." Women fall in love in prison, too, and may change their whole identity around sexuality.

"I also think they're judged more harshly than men," she says. "In general, they receive harsher sentences."

Male hierarchies abound in the criminal justice system, including administrative hierarchies and the chain of command among prison guards. Women and prisoners hold the lowest positions. And, from coast to coast, male guards rape female prisoners with impunity.[50]

Three-quarters of women prisoners are survivors of domestic violence. Many have been imprisoned for self-defense against a husband or boyfriend. In some instances the police arrive at the scene of a domestic violence situation and arrest the *victim.* Many women get arrested because their husbands or boyfriends were involved in the drug trade.[51]

The only female inmates in Oakdale are those in need of specialized medical care. Most of the time, that means pregnancy. Groups of pregnant women can be seen shuffling down the hallways or sitting in the chapel, dressed in navy blue surgical scrubs. When their baby is born, it will be given to family while the mother serves out her sentence; if no member is deemed fit to raise the child, the newborn is turned over to social services for placement in foster care. (In succeeding years, women will no longer be incarcerated at Oakdale, even for medical care).

"Unfortunately, neither the Federal Bureau of Prisons nor any state department of corrections actually attempts to keep families together," adds writer and prison activist Maya Schenwar.[52]

For example, women who give birth in prison are immediately separated from their babies. Up to ten percent of women enter prison pregnant. "They are not given adequate nutrition, and they often do not have the option of an abortion, even though it is supposed to be legal everywhere in the U.S.," Schenwar writes. "After her baby was born, my sister was immediately shackled to the bedposts. She was able to spend a little over a day with her daughter—though it was hard to hold the baby while chained to the bed."

For Marie-Crane Williams, a time came when she saw the issues women in prison faced, the trauma, and the fact that they were often unable to get the help they needed, and she was lightning-struck: "I realized that art alone is not enough to help these women."

It was an important realization, one that anyone involved in prison arts programs, like the Oakdale choir, might do well to reflect upon: Art can be incredibly useful and liberating. It can plant seeds and open minds. But it is not always enough.

As a result, Marie-Crane Williams and a number of her students undertook a survey at the Iowa Correctional Institute for Women in Mitchellville, asking female inmates about their most pressing issues. They worked collaboratively to identify areas that would improve the women's lives, and developed classes around issues such as motherhood, substance abuse, abusive relationships and medical care.

Each week for eleven weeks a semester, twelve University of Iowa students drive the hour and a half down Interstate 80 from Iowa City to Mitchellville to facilitate women's circles devoted to the development of healthy relationships. Seventy-five to a hundred incarcerated women participate.

"Mental health care is terrible inside," Marie-Crane Williams says. "The prison has counselors, but there's only so much they can do. Often it's telemedicine; they see different practitioners each time. One doctor will put them on lithium, and the next will put them on something completely different. They have no control over what they take."

Inmates face depression, bipolar illness, and various types of trauma, repeated over and over again in prison. They deal with attachment differentiation issues, being unable to trust, and the aftereffects of having faced physical, mental, and sexual abuse.

"Art is great," she says. "But what they really need are tools to help them figure out what to do when they get out. They need help to begin to untangle things with their partner. They need someone to say I see you, I recognize you, I value you.'"

She wrote the curriculum for the relationships class, and art still plays a role. "We do a lot of poetry, writing, singing, and dance. By the 7th or 8th week, women begin to share stories. Inside, there's usually no space to talk about domestic violence, so it's helpful to hear that other women have been in violent relationships. And helpful to learn how to defend yourself."

The women learn that they don't have to feel ashamed. They begin to see the bigger picture, to see that they're not alone, that their experience is not unique. They made bad choices, but, as victims of trauma, they had no good choices to make.

Marie-Crane Williams and several psychologists have also developed a program for female sex offenders. The new curriculum helps them understand unhealthy behaviors, the correlation between dependency, abuse, addiction and trauma, as well as the relationship between shame, guilt and anger that triggers unhealthy thoughts and behaviors. Participants work on coping strategies, and they make a plan for employment, housing and support for after their release.

She believes the Iowa DOC is doing its best, especially the upper administration. "They're really interested in creating opportunities. In other places I've worked, like Florida, the prisons are hell on earth: no air conditioning, big warehouses, the prisoners out weeding in a hot field. Each prison is unique, of course; it depends on the warden."

"I have a lot of sympathy for Correctional Officers. There are some kind, wonderful people among them. Also, some not very nice ones. It's a very difficult job. In Mitchellville, on the night shift there are 17 people managing 600 inmates, attending to their meds, etc. It's hard. They're not prepared for everything they see. One inmate took her own eyes out. COs are not trained to deal with that kind of thing."

People hunger here, both for music and connection. For anything really that offers a chance of getting through the day, the week, one's sentence. I've come to realize the obvious. No one knows how to cope with prison. It is an immense, overpowering force, often arbitrary, sometimes abusive, and it controls our lives in the most intimate ways. You often hear people saying in tones of awe, or disgust, or amazement, "That's crazy." And it is.

— Henry

THIRTEEN

Better Out Than In

WHEN TUESDAY ROLLS AROUND, the promise of choir can make the day pop like Technicolor in a black and white world. That's so even though we're midway through the season and a sense of urgency about getting our repertoire into shape for the upcoming concerts hovers over us.

We're working on an arrangement that merges the spirituals "Sometimes I Feel Like a Motherless Child" and "Deep River."

The basses have an especially important part. Mary urges them to step up and claim their 'bassness,' to really sink into those low, low notes. The men jut out their chins and fill their chests. Then the song quiets down, following a river-like flow of dynamics.

"I want you to listen to your neighbor," Mary says. "Make sure you're blending with the people around you in terms of pitch and volume. And be sure to enunciate. Over-enunciate! Hit those consonants! The audience won't be able to hear the words, otherwise. It's as if you're standing on a stage, acting in a play—you want to project and enunciate so that the people in the farthest seats of the auditorium can hear you!"

We practice "Sittin' on the Dock of the Bay," which is coming together nicely. Then we work on "Prayer of St. Francis."

To mix things up, Mary asks us to break into small groups. We're to collectively write some new lyrics for a song called "The Earth Does Not Belong to Us." In groups of two or three, we brainstorm ideas, coming up with some rhyming couplets. There's laughter, and for some people, the creative juices really get flowing.

I sit with Terence, who is playing around with the lyrical concept that we're just travelers passing through this world. When the whole group gets back together, a few of these lyrics are shared. Mary writes them all down and will consider how to fit some of them into the final song.

Any sense of "normal" disappears pretty quickly for a convicted felon. After his trial, Keith spent three rough and peripatetic months in county jail. He was shipped to the Pattonsburg Detention Facility in Missouri, then to Bridewell Detention Facility. After about three weeks there, he went back to Des Moines for court. That was postponed and he was taken to Marshall County Jail for a couple weeks, then back to Des Moines, then to Pattonsburg, to Des Moines, and back to Pattonsburg. He came again to Des Moines, where he was sentenced, then it was back to Marshall County for a week, then Des Moines, and from there to Oakdale.

At the time, Polk County jail couldn't hold all the inmates sent there, but Keith also believes that some of the traveling was due to the fact that it was disorienting and helped to increase the County Attorney's conviction rate.

This may be an example of what scholar William Stuntz is talking about when he says our justice system suffers from "procedural prejudice." There's too much red tape, too much tying of the judge's hands. Stuntz believes we should go into court with an understanding of what a crime is and what justice is like, and then let common sense and compassion take over. [53]

In other words, mercy and true justice—a blending of compassion and reason—are what are required in our correctional system, not simple, blind procedural fairness.

The fact that many defendants cannot afford bail, for example, perpetuates a cycle of poverty and jail time. It's basically imprisoning people for being poor, even for things like traffic tickets and court fees.

Anyway, once Keith got to Oakdale, things settled down for him. Exercising in the courtyard for an hour every other day was a great stress reliever. He had come to prison with some money, so he was able to call family. And buy things like coffee.

Still, in the early days, he sometimes felt like he was going crazy: coming off of drugs, allowed out of his room for only an hour or two a day, his interaction with others limited. It was his passion for poetry, he says, that allowed him to process his emotions, offering him another identity besides that of former addict, prisoner offender, or 'societal nuisance.'

"Writing has always given me a sense of who I am," he says, "and it's helped me maintain being that person through my incarceration, at the same time helping me change for the better."

He could, he felt, handle whatever came his way. If he didn't look for trouble, he wouldn't find it. Sure, violence, drugs, and rape existed in prison, especially at the higher security prisons. But not, he figured, the kind of thing you saw in a movie like "American History X."

And after being placed in General Population, things got easier. He wasn't locked in a cell 20 hours a day. He had use of the library, the yard, and the gym. Reading and writing poetry kept him sane. Calling home helped, but only for the duration of a 20-minute phone call. He read and he ate: food the state provided, plus what he was able to purchase from the commissary—ramen noodles, summer sausage, cheese spread, chips. Weighing 156 when he came in, over the next few months he gained 40 pounds.

As he understood it, prisoners who made up the General Population at Oakdale either had short sentences and would be released soon, long sentences and weren't eligible for treatment for a few years or longer, or were seen to be decent workers and docile in nature, and so were folded into the work force at Oakdale.

Having a job helped move you up the level system. At Oakdale in 2014, maximum pay was 53 cents an hour. The lowest rate in the state system was 24 cents an hour. (In 2017, it's 60 cents an hour.) Some prisons had specialized jobs, such as woodworking or screen-printing that allowed a person to make a little more. Other common jobs included working in the laundry, kitchen or library, ironing medical scrubs, custodial work, maintenance, or grounds crew. Some inmates arose at 5 a.m. to work in food service.

The Prison Policy Initiative asserts that perpetually low wages in prison are problematic and need to be seen in light of the increasing expenses the incarcerated face, both inside and after release. With little savings, it can be difficult to afford living expenses after release. Their success "depends largely on financial stability, which is undermined by low wages, nickel-and-diming through 'user fees,' mandatory deductions, and work that does little to prepare them for work outside of prisons."[54]

Keith's first job was to escort inmates who could participate in activities, like gym or chapel, but who were not allowed off-unit alone. The position implied a degree of trust. The better jobs, Keith understood, went to those who already had connections. Much like life on the outside.

A percentage of the money an inmate earned went to their gate fee— $100—imposed when they were paroled or discharged. Another percentage was taken out for restitution/fines, and there might be additional deductions for child support. You could keep what was left, and once everything was paid off, you received the entire paycheck, and could either save it or spend it.

Keith didn't associate with others much at first. It was, he decided, better to get the lay of the land. You came into prison with two things, he told himself—your case and your word. Lie about your case, and you lost the value of your word. So he ignored people who lied to him about why they were in prison; he could pretty much tell when someone was lying. The people who told the truth he would at least acknowledge. It didn't mean he'd hang out with them, but they gained more respect from him than somebody who lied.

He tried to keep his interactions with others friendly. You couldn't know if someone was having a bad day, so it was best to keep to yourself, or a small group, and not tangle with anyone. As you moved up the level system, it quieted down, and people got along better. Everybody serves their time in their own way, and it was easier to get along with people who served theirs in a way similar to yours.

Anyway, he hadn't come to prison to make friends.

Keith may not have thought much about the fact that other countries have strikingly different approaches than the U.S. does when it comes to treatment of prisoners and success in rehabilitation. Norway's Halden-Fengsel Prison, for example, has been called the world's most humane maximum-security prison.

That facility is located in the south of Norway, just over the border from Sweden, inland from the North Sea. It's surrounded by birch forest. You'll find no razor wire, no electric fences, and no towers with snipers.

What you will find is plenty of access to sunlight and fresh air. The architectural design of the prison encourages stability. A large wall encircles the facility, but the prison emphasizes dynamic security, the idea that interpersonal relationships between staff and inmates are the primary factor in maintaining safety. Staff members receive thorough training, with an emphasis on establishing an atmosphere of "normalcy."

Unlike the dining system in most American prisons, or at least as Patrick and Keith describe it, Halden allows inmates to cook nourishing food for themselves. They stay in individual rooms. Guards and inmates eat and play sports together. Assaults on guards are unheard of and solitary confinement is rarely used. When conflicts erupt between inmates, other inmates and chaplains sit down with them and mediate.

The Norwegian Correctional Service makes a reintegration guarantee to all released inmates, securing them a home, a job and access to a social network. Let me say that again. Each released inmate is *guaranteed* a home and a job. What kind of Scandinavian socialist craziness is this?

'Better out than in' is the Correctional Service's unofficial motto. Guards are taught that treating inmates humanely is something they should do not for the inmates but for themselves. Officer Ragnar Kristoffersen says, "If you treat people badly, it's a reflection on yourself." Harsh treatment of inmates will, he believes, ripple outward into the officers' lives, affecting their self-image, their families, even the country as a whole. [55]

Are there lessons we can learn from Norway? Absolutely. But what will need to change in the U.S. is the focus on retribution as opposed to restoration.

It wasn't always this way. As part of his "war on crime," President Johnson tasked a commission on justice with studying the conditions of filled-to-overflowing U.S. prisons. Their 1967 report, "The Challenge of Crime in a Free Society," suggested that many correctional facilities were antithetical to rehabilitation: "Life in many institutions is at best barren and futile, at worst unspeakably brutal and degrading." [56]

Referring to inmates, the report noted, "The conditions in which they live are the poorest possible preparation for their successful reentry into society, and often merely reinforce in them a pattern of manipulation and destructiveness."

The commission put forward a vision for prisons much like that of Halden in Norway. In the mid-1970s, the U.S. Bureau of Prisons built several facilities designed to reflect these practices. These so-called Metropolitan Correctional Centers were "new generation" institutions. Groups of 44 prisoners lived in self-contained units in which "all of the single-inmate cells (with wooden doors meant to reduce both noise and cost) opened onto a day room, where they ate, socialized and met with visitors or counselors, minimizing the need for moving inmates outside the unit."

"All the prisoners spent the entire day outside their cells with a single unarmed correctional officer in an environment meant to diminish the sense of institutionalization and its attendant psychological stresses, with wooden and upholstered furniture, desks in the cells, porcelain toilets, exposed light fixtures, brightly colored walls, skylights and carpeted floors."

But a shift had taken place in both public opinion and political commitment by the time the centers opened. Much of this backlash can be traced to the writings of Robert Martinson, a sociologist at the City University of New York, who analyzed data about the impact of rehabilitation programs on recidivism. [57]Despite the fact that half the programs did show evidence of effectiveness, Martinson's 1974 article concluded that no program showed consistent results.

The paper was trotted out by the media and by politicians, who seized on the idea that "nothing works" in regard to prisoner rehabilitation.

This research was quickly challenged; a 1975 analysis by another sociologist criticized Martinson's choice to overlook successful programs. And by 1979, Martinson himself had published another paper withdrawing his previous conclusion, declaring that some treatment programs *do* have an appreciable effect on recidivism.

The problem was that, by then, the "nothing works" narrative was firmly entrenched. In 1984, a Senate report calling for more stringent sentencing guidelines cited Martinson's 1974 paper, without acknowledging his later reversal. Get-tough-on-crime policies sprouted in Congress and state legislatures.

Today, around 350 Metropolitan Correctional Center-type facilities still exist, making up less than seven percent of the incarceration sites in the United States. They're mostly county-level, pretrial jails. Data has shown that they have lower levels of violence among inmates and against guards, and reduced recidivism.

Prison is big business, a multi-million or billion dollar industry that profits from the incarceration of human beings. No matter what the public is told about decreasing prison populations, the reality is that the number of inmates grows ever larger and the system continues to expand to accommodate them, them and the ones that will follow. There is little incentive to reduce recidivism in the face of enterprise for profit.

— *Patrick*

FOURTEEN

When You Go Missing

EVERETT IS IN A talkative mood.

"The food was bad last night," he tells me before rehearsal. "They serve meals on a five-week cycle, see? And sometimes we just get hit with bad food. Last night the food was terrible. But we've got a microwave up on Unit Four, and a bunch of us mixed together some ramen noodles, some cheese and lunchmeat, and we had a great time."

"How's your diet going?" I ask him. "Your ab exercises?" I know he's had health problems, and struggles with his weight.

"You mean my flab exercises?" He smiles. "I'm still working at it."

Everett drinks a lot of water, so he's up all night peeing. He rooms with three other guys, and they don't mind, he says, if it's just pee. He's taking a med that makes the other one smelly, though.

Everett is someone with whom I've become comfortable over the course of several seasons, and he's become comfortable with me. As we chat between songs, he tells me about his job. Assigned to type up the classifying info for prisoners coming into Oakdale, he gets to know many of the new guys. They're missing their families, they're missing their mothers, some are missing their dogs. Many come to him for advice; Everett talks to them and tries to make them feel better. Insiders are not supposed to touch each other, but sometimes these new arrivals start to cry, and just latch on to him. He's known as 'Pawpaw' on the unit, a kind of parental figure.

He also plays guitar for the Spanish church service on Sundays, so he's learning something about Mexican styles of music. "More people from Mexico are coming into prison these days," he tells me. "And not only from Mexico. The man I was learning Swahili from was sent back to Kenya. He was happy to go, because he said no one would bother him there."

Maybe it's coincidence, but the more I become involved with prisoners, the more I encounter issues of crime and punishment popping up in front of me everywhere: discussions of prison reform in the news, conversations overheard between people who have loved ones inside.

One weekend I'm on my way to Chicago to give a reading from my first book, a just-published memoir, when a group of four or five men board the bus I'm on. Like many Greyhound passengers, they look a bit down on their luck, and as if they had a story to tell. The only difference is that these men are wearing matching sweatshirts and jeans, and one of them complains about the crowded conditions of the bus. With no single seats left, every passenger has to share a double seat.

"Shit, man, what is this? I feel like I'm in a cell," the man who slides into the seat next to me says to one of his companions across the aisle. I turn to the window and hunker into my book. My quickly formed impression pegs him as a perpetually negative kind of guy. What could we possibly have in common? Thus do our quick prejudices betray us.

Something leads to a break in the ice, though, some question about the arrival time at one of our destinations, an innocuous exchange between strangers on a bus. We start to talk, and he turns out to be friendly, funny, and smart. Besides this, he has just gotten out of the Illinois state prison after ten years inside. *This morning.*

As we speak, I'm able to put his actions into context. His tough talk is likely for the benefit of the other recently released inmates. They're probably guys he doesn't know well, but with whom he has shared an intense experience, as well as a release date.

I tell him that I sing with prisoners, and also that I've just written a book, and am on my way to do some readings.

"Like Stephen King? Dean Koontz?" he asks.

"Nothing that big."

"Man, I could write a book about what I saw inside. Guys cutting off their little fingers. Even cutting off their thingies. Last week a lady officer got punched in the face, her glasses broke and the glass went into her eye. Crazy shit."

He's muscular, and at first glance he appears emotionally hardened. But he's not so tough that he can't share his anxiety with me about reemerging into the world. At the Walmart this morning, the crowds and the size of the place had gotten to him; he'd had to beat a hasty retreat. Now, on the bus, too, he feels anxious. He can't wait to get home; his Italian mother has been cooking all day.

"I'm going to have pasta 'til I can't eat any more, and a steak. Then I'm going to sit in my parents' Jacuzzi."

"It's the little things, you know? The little things I'm looking forward to. Like being able to walk barefoot on plush carpeting. Or trees. Fresh air. A Big Mac. Not having to share a cell with someone who snores and farts all night long."

His name is Jimmy. He has an 11-year old daughter, and he's dearly looking forward to reconnecting with her.

"What's her name?"

"Carmella."

"A good Italian name. Wasn't that Tony Soprano's wife's name?"

"Yeah," he laughs. "She's bossy, too."

He tells me he's feeling a little dizzy and I offer him some water.

"No, I'm OK."

But the moment allows him to wax rhetorical. "You know, the doctors inside don't do shit. You go to the dentist and instead of filling a cavity, they just pull the tooth. It's like that all around. The taxpayer is getting ripped off, 'cause they're putting a lot of money into prisons, but where is the money going? The prisoners sure don't see any benefit."

I realize that I can ask this fleeting acquaintance questions I couldn't easily ask of choir members. Were you angry when you went in? Was there a moment when you realized you had to get your act together? Or did it happen gradually?

He's happy to talk.

"I guess I was pretty pissed off, in the beginning. But over time, you grow." He'd been involved with drugs as a younger man, and lets slip hints at gang association. When he takes off his jacket his forearms dazzle with colorful tattoos spread over every inch of skin.

"But I listened to all the old guys in there who had something to teach. You know what they say, you can't teach somebody if they don't want to learn. But I soaked up the wisdom of those guys who had been in there a long time."

"I was 140 pounds when I went in. Now, I'm 220," he laughs. "Nothing to do except pump iron and eat. I also had cancer while I was inside. Lost one of my lungs. But I'm cancer-free now. I must be a fucking idiot to buy these cigarettes." He points to the pack he had bought before getting on the bus, one loose cigarette in his hand, as he waits for the bus to stop so he can get in another smoke break. "Actually, I haven't smoked in years. But I think it's the anxiety. I just want to smoke one."

He's going to be working with his uncle who has a landscaping business in Chicago. Inside, he earned an associate's degree in business management. It seems his time has not been misspent.

"I just kept my head down, kept out of other people's shit. You can survive. I got my GED, then my associate's degree."

In all of this, and in having a place to stay and a job waiting for him, he's fortunate. Many people coming out of prison don't have this kind of support system. I listen to his compatriots talk from the seats behind us. Their conversation ranges over whom they knew in the 'hood, fights they had once upon a time, and street gossip. Jimmy is older, 38, and tells me he's matured.

At the next stop, Naperville, he steps off to have his smoke, then climbs back on and settles himself in his seat. Before pulling out, the bus driver asks if any of the passengers are still off the bus, if anyone is missing?

Jimmy laughs. He's been making mafia jokes all along, playing up his Italian heritage.

"It's like Johnny the Fish used to say, 'When you go missing, you stay missing.'"

Oakdale was originally a psychiatric facility and its current status still includes a medical and psychiatric orientation. Commonly held images of psych facilities often loom forebodingly as gray and enervating and maybe a little bit spooky—think 'Arkham Asylum' in the Batman comics. I think this is so because we fear what we might become, the potential in all of us, as human beings, to go off the rails. On the other hand, this fluidity also portends the possibility of improvement and renewed balance.

Inmates entering the prison system face all sorts of terrible health issues. Dr. Harbans Deol, director of medical services at Oakdale, tells me that many prisoners are diabetic, or deal with hypertension. A few may be paraplegic; some are in need of abdominal surgery. A Department of

Justice report notes that in 2011–12, half of state and federal prisoners and local jail inmates reported ever having a chronic condition.[58] (Chronic conditions include cancer, high blood pressure, stroke-related problems, diabetes, heart-related problems, kidney-related problems, arthritis, asthma, and cirrhosis of the liver.)

And always, there's a lot of mental illness.

Deol's staff watches studiously for suicide attempts, especially in the first thirty days of incarceration.

Add to this the fact that dementia is increasing in Iowa's prisons due to an aging inmate population, and even though the overall number of incarcerated is slightly declining, the number of seriously mentally ill inmates remains high.[59]

In Iowa this percentage is at 25 to 30 percent; the national average is 18 to 20 percent. (The seeming disparity is because Iowa includes more issues in the definition of mental illness than some states.)

Another report notes that half of the people incarcerated in prisons and two-thirds of those in jails had either "serious psychological distress," or a history of mental health problems.[60] Yet only about a third of those reporting serious psychological distress were currently receiving treatment. It's sad to say, but America's prisons have become *de facto* warehouses for people with mental health challenges.

We can trace some of the origins of this trend to the mid-20th century, when abuses within mental institutions in the U.S. reached a peak. Beginning in the early 1970s, mental health patients began to be systematically transferred out of institutions in many states and into community programs, a process known as 'deinstitutionalization.'[61]

President Reagan was a big proponent of this idea that mentally ill patients should be released into the community. New medications were being developed at the time, which led to a hope that the mentally ill could function on their own. A number of institutions closed.

But the movement went too far. Lack of treatment or assistance for many low-income people with mental health issues—even something as simple as not having someone remind them to take their meds—often led to erratic behavior, and an encounter with police could result in jail time.

Putting people in jail and prison became the state's strategy for dealing with a health crisis created by drug use and dependency—75 percent of mental health cases involve substance abuse.

The good news is that many of these inmates can function well once their illness is addressed, Deol says. A typical treatment protocol relies on psychiatric medication, working with a psychologist—which may include cognitive therapy or anger management—and helping a patient understand their disease process. It can take four to six weeks to stabilize a patient's condition when he or she comes in. Though probably, Deol says, they'll be taking meds for the rest of their lives.

I wonder about this reliance on medications. I'm no expert, but having had friends who've dealt with depression through the use of medication and been stymied by their side effects, I worry about the overuse of psychiatric meds. As essayist Rebecca Solnit puts it, "People undergo losses and ordeals that would make any sane person sad, and then we say if you feel sad you're crazy or sick and should be medicated."[62]

On the other hand, I understand that many psychiatric issues can and need to be addressed through meds, and I wouldn't want to begrudge anyone improvement in their condition. Some insiders are dealing with conditions like schizophrenia, and for that, certainly, meds are a necessity. Besides which, certain options (like taking a walk in the woods to improve your mood) are just not available in prison.

A major challenge faced by the DOC *is* a lack of resources, Deol says. There's a shortage of psychiatrists, for one thing. "If we had all the resources we needed, what measures would I like to see taken?" he asks. "Nicer housing, more programming, more time outdoors. Staff spending more time with inmates. These things work."

Deol insists the food is good in prison; he says the staff eats the same food as the inmates. This doesn't quite jibe with what several insiders have told me. It could be a matter of perspective, an Oakdale administrator putting a positive spin on things. Or it could be insiders complaining without reason. It's hard to know, though I tend to trust the judgment of insiders who have been eating the food for years.

There are success stories at Oakdale when it comes to treatment of mental illness, though they don't always receive attention. Deol recalls one patient who was given to swallowing things, anything he could get his hands on. The man had numerous visits with a psychiatrist, and with a doctor, and eventually the issue was brought under control.

Another case involved a high-profile murderer who came to Oakdale. The man had smiled in his newspaper photo and people thought it showed a lack of remorse. But, Deol says, it was just that the man was seriously mentally ill. "We put him on meds and later his mother told me that this was the best level of functioning she'd ever seen him at. He asked me why he had to come to prison to get the treatment he needed."

In 1955, there was one psychiatric bed for every 300 Americans. In 2005 it was one for every 3000. I wish I could report that this is because we're becoming healthier as a nation, but statistics don't bear that out.

"It would be good," Deol muses, "if we had more mental health beds in the community, so some folks didn't have to go to prison."

Unfortunately, it looks like that's unlikely to happen any time soon. In 2015, the governor of Iowa announced intentions to close two major mental health facilities in a cost-saving measure, those in Clarinda and Mt. Pleasant.

This, in a state the Treatment Advocacy Center ranks last in terms of mental health beds available for citizens. Iowa has just 64 beds for mental health patients, translating to two beds for every 100,000 Iowans.[63]

Prison images continue to surface for me in the night, whales rising from the deep. In this dream, I'm a prisoner, standing in line with others, waiting to receive my tray of food. I feel all my flaws, my insecurities, acutely, and imagine that others can perceive them, too. One young man comes up behind me and knocks the tray out of my hands; my meal splashes onto the concrete floor.

How should I react? One part of me impulsively wants to smack him over the head with the tray. Another part decides not to retaliate, and not to tell the authorities— what good would it do? It would only perpetuate a cycle.

Instead, I start to talk with the man, and learn that he has lost a son. When I awake, what lingers is a feeling—of how tremendously vulnerable we all are.

FIFTEEN

Places Not Made of Stone

FOR SOME AMERICANS, PRISON functions as a metaphorical lockbox into which they can project their fear and anger about crime and criminals, and then resort to 'out of sight, out of mind' thinking. This may owe something to the depiction of prisons in film. Reel upon reel of celluloid have lit up America's movie screens, reflecting perceptions of the justice system over many decades. *I am a Fugitive from a Chain Gang. 20,000 Years in Sing Sing. Caged Fury. The Concrete Jungle. Papillon. Midnight Express. The Green Mile.*

In *The Defiant Ones*, for example, Tony Curtis and Sidney Poitier escape from jail chained to and resentful of each other, and America's thorny 1960s race issues are played out in metaphorical *and* literal terms, as the pair learn to cooperate in order to survive. I particularly remember the scene, early in the film, in which, simmering with mutual resentment, they fight each other. Because they're chained together, each time one knocks the other down, both are pulled to the ground. Could there be a more potent, poignant metaphor for our lives and fates together as Americans?

Prisoners have often been portrayed in film either as hardened, remorseless sociopaths, or idealized savants. Television, too, with shows like *COPS*, offers a slanted commentary on crime, stoking public fear and outrage and the demand for harsher prison terms in a sensational way. Vengeance, vigilante justice, and violence are themes that sell advertising, but they also subtly shape the way we think.

And yet, most Americans have never visited a prison, never interacted with prisoners or parolees. Our perception of life inside is, for the most part, one big projection, in every sense of the word.

However, one film making the case for prison being a place where, despite oppressive conditions, one's humanity can be cultivated, is *The Shawshank Redemption*, based on a Stephen King story. You probably know it: its main character, accountant Andy Dufresne, played by Tim Robbins, is wrongly imprisoned and faces institutional inertia and corruption. At night he quietly chisels a tunnel to freedom through his cell wall, the opening to which he hides behind a pinup poster of Rita Hayworth. During the day he works to improve fellow prisoners' lives, organizing a library, offering educational opportunities.

One scene is particularly moving. It's the one where Dufresne locks himself in the warden's office and, selecting an opera record from albums donated to the new prison library, proceeds to broadcast an aria over the PA system and into the prison yard. As the needle drops, the music—'Canzonetta sull'aria' from Mozart's "Marriage of Figaro" — floats above the courtyard, and we see prisoners stop what they're doing, pause, turn their faces upward, and listen.

The grinding routine is disrupted; for a moment these men are allowed entry into another world. Time seems to slow. Beauty appears, all of a sudden, and it's that much sweeter because it's forbidden.

Then the COs break down the door to the warden's office and bring Dufresne to heel. The incident costs him time *in the hole*, but the moment of transcendence seems to have been worth it.

It's significant that the scene features music as a key to inner freedom. I've seen similar expressions on the faces of men standing next to me in choir.

"There are places in the world not made out of stone," Dufresne explains to his friends once he's out of solitary.

"Something inside they can't get to, that they can't take away from you."

Patrick originally heard about the choir from one of his cellmates. His initial response was to tease the cellmate, suggesting that the only reason he was there was to ogle the female volunteers. Participation in activities like the choir, Patrick had thought, was not worthy of respect from the so-called 'hardcore' criminals. And this was important to him.

As the spring concert last year drew nearer, however, his roommate kept up the pressure to attend. So on the night of our performance for inmates, Patrick found himself sitting in the gym, perched on a folding chair, waiting for the music to begin.

And, surprise, surprise, the choir was good! Dr. Cohen had taken a ragtag group of volunteers and inmates and turned them into a real singing group. Patrick watched the volunteers and was impressed with how freely they interacted with the insiders.

Shortly afterwards, Mary Cohen announced she was starting a songwriter's workshop to be held during the choir's summer break. Patrick had been interested in writing songs for a while; he decided to get involved. By the end of the summer, Cohen had set some of Patrick's lyrics to music and encouraged him to allow the choir to perform the resulting song, "Tapestry", at the winter concert. That was the final straw. Throwing caution to the wind, when the choir started up again in the fall, he signed on to sing.

We begin to sit next to each other in the tenor section. I like him immediately. He's an intelligent and wryly funny man. Grayish-brown hair tumbles down his back, framing a worn rugged face. His singing voice is chalky and rough.

As a new piece of music is handed out, we admire the cover page together. It looks like an old explorer's map or lithograph. There are clouds with puffed-out cheeks blowing the wind ahead of them, hinting at travel, adventure, escape into uncharted territory.

"There should be an 'x' and a sign that says 'here there be dragons.'"

"I know, right?"

Patrick's traveling days may be over for now, but his imagination continues to soar. He's always writing, and some of the choir's most memorable songs in the coming days will be written by him.

His song "Grain of Sand" sums up his attitude about coping with prison. He says, "There are days when we feel like the system is just trying to grind us up. It's a big machine, and one little thing can happen that can bring all of that to a screeching halt. Sometimes it's a CO knowing me by name and saying hello. You know, it can frame everything that they tried to do to dehumanize us and do away with it. So whether it's incidents, or people, that are the grains of sand, the song is basically a call for somebody to intervene from time to time in our lives, in order to keep us from being processed by this place."[64]

There's power in a grain of sand which, once a mountain lofty and imposing,
Now reduced you see scattered cross some distant land.

Behold man's mightiest machine with surface cold, metallic gleam,
And giant parts with power strong, the toughest thing man's ever seen.
But then, a grain of sand slips in beneath machine's protective skin
And travels quickly to its core, creating an enormous din.
Some massive gears begin to creak and swiftly flowing fluids leak;
Then warning lights come brightly on as power drops from strong
to weak.
The great machine cries out in pain and struggles to run on, in vain;
Its awesome power come to naught disrupted by one tiny grain.
Within this tale a moral lies, 'bout all such things that men devise:
A weakness has each great machine, regardless of its weight or size.
So hear me now my heartfelt plea; held captive by the DOC
I'm caught within their great machine,
Please be a grain of sand for me!

Today is one of Colin's final rehearsals. Our volunteer piano accompanist, Colin is a senior at the university majoring in piano performance and music education, and the nicest kid. He's spent a lot of time helping insiders write songs. He'll be graduating soon, and has signed up for the Peace Corps. He's headed for Kenya. He and I have become friends and we often trade jokes on our way in and out of the prison.

"Why couldn't Beethoven find his teacher?"

"Because he was Haydn." Get it?

Colin put great effort into learning the piano part for each song. His self-deprecating sense of humor has endeared him to many. As a show of solidarity, several of us attended his senior piano recital at the university. Outsider choir members often make the effort to be there for each other's significant events. We look forward to the day when we can be there for released insiders in this way, too.

Mary invites us to sign a thank you card for Colin. As we pass it down the line of singers, each person scrawls their name and their good wishes. And then we go around the circle and voice our appreciation.

"Thanks, Colin, and all the outsiders," one of the insiders begins, "for not considering us disposable."

Others chime in. "God bless you on your journey."

"Fare thee well."

"Your biggest gift was simply being with us. You didn't try to impose anything on us, though we learned a lot from you. Just being here, showing up, was the most important thing."

"You made me smile."

The new accompanist pipes up: "I have big shoes to fill."

Colin's eyes are brimming with tears. "I love you all. And this has been the greatest experience of community I've had in my college years. So, thank you."

As we leave the prison, Colin and I walk together and he fills me in on his travel preparations. When he arrives in Kenya, he'll be near the border with Uganda. He's concerned about malaria, but he's taking his prophylactic medicines so he won't get sick.

No, he hasn't learned any Swahili yet.

Yes, his parents have been very supportive.

Yes. He'll miss the choir very much.

Listening to people thank Colin puts me in mind of something. It takes me a little while to figure out what, but finally I realize: in our collective contributions we're something like a Greek Chorus. The Greek Chorus, of course, is the communal body that, in Greek drama, observes and comments on the actions of actors on the stage. The rhythm of the chorus' lines is designed to pull the audience in on a sensory level. Sophocles and Aristophanes utilized the device in most of their tragedies. Woody Allen did, too, in "Mighty Aphrodite."

The Greeks believed that music was a gift from the gods. They also felt that punishment was intended to penalize hubris—"the failure to behave as befits one's position in the social hierarchy." [65] As such it served the function of *kolasis,* or chastisement, teaching people their proper place. I think this can be read not so much about being stuck in place—a kind of class immobility—as about remembering who you are, supported by those around you.

In other words (if we follow the thread of this metaphor further), when we remember who we are—members of society deserving of dignity—or are *re-membered* by those around us, we're much less likely to pursue actions that disrupt the community.

I guess a question may arise, though, within the parameters of this exercise. Are we, like characters in a Greek tragedy, at the mercy of forces greater than ourselves, forces of fate, character, or social condemnation? Do our fatal flaws, our hubris, condemn us to immovable destinies? Or do we have a choice about the future?

It's very important that the inmates remain busy, and have a sense of purpose. The hardest part of incarceration is fighting boredom. Boredom leads to problems.

— Oakdale warden Jim McKinney

SIXTEEN

A Portal of Awesomeness

THE WIND WHIPS ALONG the road in front of the prison. Snow forms sleeves on the tree branches, coats the walls, and rests in curlicues on razor wire. Winter has well and truly come to Oakdale.

Tonight we'll hold our first concert of the semester, before a group of Oakdale inmates. Most of the time, the vast echoing gymnasium is full of men shooting hoops or pumping iron. Now, in the hour before our performance, it's quiet.

As we arrive, chairs are being trotted out and the sound system set up. Young tenor Jack weaves around the tenor section. "I've got a sore throat tonight, so I can't really sing," he says.

"It's the best he's sounded all year," Terence cracks.

Jack laughs and shrugs. He's excited to take part, anyway.

There's a little time before the concert begins. After warm-ups and some touchups on a few of the pieces, Mary has us break into small groups for discussion. Many insiders have little experience with such things, and so this kind of exercise sometimes devolves into simply hanging out and bantering.

Some of the conversations deepen, though. We start out in groups of six or seven, but the introverts among us soon drift to the side. I introduce myself to a man I haven't spoken with before. With his handlebar mustache and leathery skin, he looks like an extra in a Western movie.

"Charles?" I look at his ID badge.

"Chip," he replies.

What about the theme of this concert, "Come Walk with Us?" I ask, following Mary's prompt. "I think… I think it's about loving everybody," the man opines. "We've got to love one another, no matter who they are."

"I like that," I say. "To me, it's about moving forward together, making sure no one in society gets left behind."

"That sounds good." We smile at each other.

The last of the inmate concert guests is ushered into the gym and they take their seats. Several are in wheelchairs. A few slouch in the back, looking bored.

Chip and I shake hands, and make our way back to our sections.

Tyrone, a thoughtful young white insider with a Hebrew inscription tattooed on his forearm, steps to the microphone to open the show and welcome the audience. "You know, it was really hard for me to be here tonight, since a lot of things have changed this year. My mother taught me a lot about faith and love and keeping commitments, so I thank you guys for being here. This is about honoring a commitment, and so I want to thank the choir for showing up and honoring a commitment to us."

As the audience applauds, Brett steps up and introduces the arrangement of "Motherless Child/Deep River."

"The lyrics of this song are like a deep river flowing on," he begins. "I was raised not too far from the Mississippi, and it had a huge impact on my life. When I was young, I swam and went boating and camped on the banks of that mighty Mississippi. I watched the sun rise and set many times on that river. When I was sad or lonely, the river brought me tranquility."

"These lyrics mean a lot to me. I never knew my father; he left us when I was a few days old, and all I have are pictures. Sometimes I wonder how things might've been different. But then again, things happen for a reason. Thank you for attending."

Brett's words have captured everyone's attention. Now Mary steps onto the podium, faces us, and mouths the words "Watch me." She stretches her cheek muscles and opens her eyes wide, reminding us to smile.

We begin to sing.

The piano offers simple, hopeful arpeggios. Our voices blend into a greater-than-parts whole, tapping into the melancholic essence of the first part of the song, and the redemptive depth of the second.

Sometimes I feel like a motherless child.
Deep river, Lord.

Sometimes I feel like a motherless child.
My home is over Jordan.

The basses claim their "bassness," puffing out their chests. As they sing, *I feel like a motherless child,* poignancy fills the room.

Oh, don't you want to go to that promised land? In response, the pure high descant of female voices is comforting.

A reverent hush radiates from the audience when we finish, followed by sustained applause. We look around at each other. Mary gives us a thumbs-up and mouths the words, "Good job!"

Now Patrick steps to the mic to introduce his song. Patrick, who laughed at the idea of joining the choir, whose past is dark with guns and drugs, now seems a different man.

"Good evening. I'd like to give you a little background about the next song that we're going to do. My friend here collaborated on this song with me." He points to an inmate standing next to him. "We have a lot in common. We're both attractive young men in the prime of life." The audience laughs. "We both have fashionable haircuts." More laughter. "And we both chose to vacation here at the ever-popular Oakdale Spa and Resort."

Patrick smiles as we launch into "Tapestry," and he continues to smile throughout the choir's rendition of his song. It, too, goes well.

Karletta comes forward: "Here's how this next song came about. Dr. Cohen gave us the opportunity to write new lyrics to a song, called 'The Earth Does Not Belong to Us.' So with partners and small groups we discussed the meaning of the original lyrics, and we wrote some new lyrics. Then we gathered to share what we had written."

"In this process of sharing, we noticed a couple of recurring themes. Peace, and the earth's role in providing that peace. Cycles and patterns and the significance of the past. Giving thanks for the gifts of the earth. And the fact that, because of our interactions with each other and our environment, we are all connected."

"And if we think in terms of the relationships in that connection, we'll ultimately be more at peace with each other."

The choir rises and sings:

The earth does not belong to us, but we belong to the earth.
This radiant sphere of green and blue, our home and place of birth.
The web of life connects us all, each strand its vital role
For what affects a single one, affects the living whole.

I glance at my fellow tenors. They're all earnestly singing, and maybe because of all the buildup and the fact that things are going so well, suddenly everything slips away from me but a sense of joy. Instead of excitement, I feel peace. In my mind, there's no preoccupation, no ego chatter, just the ecstasy of creating music together. It's a beautiful thing. I can't speak for my fellow singers, but some of them certainly seem to be *in the flow,* too.

A young white insider named Banning steps up and introduces a song he's written for his young daughter. Emphasizing how much he loves her, and how much he's looking forward to getting to know her, he says it's important that she understands he wants to be there for her, but for now, he can't. His voice catches as he speaks, and he tears up.

So little and so sweet, Never have I met you, Not that I don't want to, I may not be there, But in my dreams I'm with you, and we have time to share.

A few insiders in the audience seem abashed at the sentiment of love and unity we're presenting. Is this OK? Can we let our guard down? Others join in wholeheartedly, adding to the atmosphere. Several prisoners clap and sway.

"Prayer of St. Francis," "All Things Bright and Beautiful," "Breathe Holy Breath"—I have to say that we shine on all of these. As the concert winds to an end, Mary thanks the crowd for their attention, and invites those gathered here to consider joining the choir next year. We bask in the glow of the applause.

Then the choir members stretch out around the gymnasium, forming a receiving line. Audience members walk up and congratulate us, one by one. I look into the eyes of thirty different men.

It's a diverse crowd. Some attendees have come over from the psych ward. You can see etched into some of these faces the outlines of a series of mistakes made; you can almost sense how some people end up here because of an uncertainty about how to live. One young man is shy and confused, barely able to meet my gaze. Others are happy for the chance to say hello, to thank us for the performance. There was energy created during the concert, and they want to connect.

Thank you. Thank you. Thank you for coming.

The outside choir members line up to leave the gymnasium. Chatting excitedly, we head down the hall toward the main door, and spill into the parking lot, embracing a feeling of accomplishment as we breathe in the crisp night air.

And after putting away the chairs, the inside singers walk through the corridor, slapping each other on the back and receiving congratulations from other inmates.

One by one, they retire to their cells.

The next week's rehearsal is scheduled the day before the larger concert, when we'll be performing for an audience from the community. We trade notes on last week's performance and discuss what we can do better for this next one.

Jen stands and says, "I just want to go on record to say that I think the song "Deep River/Motherless Child" opened up a portal of awesomeness. It was so good. We were really in the zone on that one." There are murmurs of agreement.

People offer other suggestions. Maria says, "After we finish a song, don't rustle your papers or throw your music down, or even move, right away. Give it a moment."

Mary agrees. "There's a space of silence before and after the music, a space which is full of energy. Let's allow the audience to feel that. Let the silence ring out."

Burt raises his hand. "Those 'choos' are just killing us. Whenever we say 'At you,' or 'but you' we have to enunciate!"

People nod their heads.

"And," someone calls out, "remember to smile!"

Paul, the curmudgeon, pipes up. "I already smiled once today."

Maria: "Then you won't have to do it again until tomorrow."

Paul: "That makes me smile."

I, too, had an adventure—a trip to the hospital for an annual visit to a specialist— one advantage to being here. I saw leafless trees, swollen streams, a reservoir, people walking around, perfectly unconscious of their freedom to do so, restaurants, highways, motorcycles and trucks, and renewed my acquaintance with manacles, shackles, and guards with guns.

— Henry

SEVENTEEN

Teaching and Learning

MARY TRACHSEL WAS STROLLING down the street in front of her house, humming a song that had been written by an insider, when her neighbor, out shoveling the sidewalk, hailed her, "Oh, I like that! What's that tune?"

It was a poignant moment: the inner, creative life of an inside singer, expressed and acknowledged on the city street, far from prison.

It was Trachsel, a University of Iowa rhetoric professor with glasses and short graying brown hair, who introduced me to the OCC, back in 2010, in a "short forms of nonfiction" class we both attended at the Iowa Summer Writing Festival. Her stories of singing with prisoners intrigued me, and that fall Lois and I signed up.

Soon after the choir began in 2009, Trachsel began helping with the writing prompts. She also produced a choir newsletter. While engaged in this work, she received repeated requests for a writing class from insiders. Her husband had done some volunteering in the prison, offering creative writing instruction. Building on this, she began to develop and facilitate a Writing Workshop (distinct from the songwriting workshop), offering writing exercises, readings, and feedback.

An outsider support contingent soon sprang up. Now, once a week, ten to twelve people, insiders and outsiders, sit at a table in one of the prison's meeting rooms, drinking coffee. (The coffee, they say, is important.) Having distributed their writing in advance, each person reads their piece aloud, and then they listen to feedback.

Attendees have cultivated reputations for being certain kinds of writers. Each member develops a personality within the group. Chester's work is 'lotiony,' smooth like massage oil. They speak of the 'Jeremyness' of a piece of writing. There are also a number of people from the mental health unit who participate. One, says Trachsel, is very, very talented.

She has witnessed a growing confidence in the participants, an excitement at being able to discuss ideas about craft and theme. The continual exploration with and explanation to each other means that writing ideas are more deeply imprinted on their consciousness.

At first Trachsel wondered whether to place constraints on what people could say or write. Patrick, for example, wrote a story as a joke, in which he got out hostile feelings toward a few officers: 'I miss you, but my aim is getting better.' And Chester wrote Hallmark-type lyrics shading into erotica.

"Some things I wouldn't copy initially, wondering whether we were crossing a line," she says. "Finally, I decided to just let go of any restrictions. Basically, participants just want to express the feeling, 'I'm a human being. I have a voice.'"

A number of genres land on the table between the coffee mugs. Young African American insider Armand wrote advice columns for a while. Keith penned a musical. Jeremy has a children's novel in the works. Memoirs abound. Fantasy is popular. And thanks to crossover between the Songwriting and Writing Workshops, poems and songs originate in one place and migrate to the other.

People work out their personal issues, sometimes obliquely, sometimes directly, on the page. In his advice column, Armand was great at introducing topics people were hesitant to talk about. He posed sensitive questions. Why is there a hierarchy in prison? Why do male prisoners badmouth women? Why do drug dealers feel superior to sex offenders? Why are all sex offenders considered the same?

Armand framed his questions in terms of how he himself used to behave: 'I know why you feel you have to badmouth women. I've been there.' This led to some poignant discussions.

As for the outsiders, their role is to listen. It's a bit different from the choir, although listening is important there as well. Workshop facilitators do occasionally offer advice. Trachsel shares one piece she originally received from her mother: 'Write when you're angry.'

She claims there's never been a scary moment. The people who show up are self-selecting, and usually not very aggressive. After all, a person has to decide how they're going to spend their time in prison. People often start out by reading books, sometimes for the first time in their lives, and writing is a logical next step.

The workshop has led to other spinoffs and organic developments. Patrick entered a national prison-writing contest. He didn't win, but he did get recognized. The Iowa City alternative newsweekly Little Village regularly publishes insiders' essays. A group called the Pen and Paper Club has sprung up, organized by insiders, sharing graphic art and poetry. One outsider regularly gives cartooning lessons.

Has Trachsel seen changes in the guys?

"I don't think in terms of behavioral changes, but in terms of how relationships develop. That's the good thing, the relationships. The administration warns against friendships, but they must know it's bound to happen."

"I'm ambivalent when people are transferred or released and move on," she says. "I'm happy, but I miss them."

Speaking of writing, one interesting aspect of the OCC is its writing component. Prompts handed out at the end of each rehearsal are taken "home" by choir members to reflect on and respond to during the week, and these responses are gathered at the following rehearsal. The voluntary exercise allows singers to muse on their experiences, share their thoughts, and develop their writing skills. Stop, reflect. This extra step in the twitchy chain between impulse and action offers an opportunity to practice an important feature in personal behavior that's sometimes missing: impulse control.

And, because each piece of writing is shared with another choir member and you get to read their comments when you get your paper back, it's another chance to interact in a thoughtful way.

In a recent prompt, members wrote about favorite songs. "More than just letters and symbols on a page, the music and message we take up becomes a part of us, to be communicated to others," one inside singer mused.

Wrote another, "The song 'Show us the Way' speaks to me as well as 'Breathe Holy Breath'. They both give me the hope of not only becoming a light in the darkness, but to also share that light with those around me. I often struggle with compassion, though at times it flows freely through me. I believe these two songs will stay with me as prayers, more than just songs. Yes, I feel these songs are like prayers drifting through the air and coming to mind when needed the most."

Another wrote, "Over a period of time it has been interesting to observe my own feelings about singing in the choir. All the things we do are both fun and work. It's like going to any other choir I have been in. Now there are people I know better than others and some I don't know now with many new members. At first I tried to know everyone but now I concentrate more on singing. What we create together here does not feel average in the end because it has the power to change its members and audiences as well as the whole prison system. I feel it has already."

"When people come together, powerful things happen. By coming together every week to create music, the wonderful interaction can produce an energy that will touch all members as well as those who listen."

This emphasis on writing is a good thing in more ways than one. Nineteen percent of adult inmates are illiterate, and up to 60 percent are functionally illiterate, that is, lacking the literacy for coping with most everyday situations. (In contrast, the national adult illiteracy rate stands at 4 percent, with up to 23 percent functionally illiterate.) Any opportunity to develop literacy skills is appreciated. Many inmates are eager to avail themselves of whatever educational opportunities become available.

Beginning in 1965, American inmates had been permitted to apply for Pell Grants in order to attend college. By 1982, more than 350 college prison programs existed, available in 90 percent of the states. There's overwhelming consensus that postsecondary education is the most successful and cost-effective way to prevent crime, say Daniel Karpowitz and Max Kenner of the Bard Prison Initiative. [66]

Of the $5.3 billion awarded in Pell Grants in 1993, only about $34 million were awarded to inmates. This represents less than 1/10 of one percent of the total grant awards. The annual Pell Grant awarded to an inmate was less than $1,300. Pells were given to education providers, not inmates, to pay for the inmates' educational expenses.

But something happened. In the 1990s, responding to political pressures to get tougher on crime, elected officials began introducing legislation to prohibit inmate tuition assistance. The Department of Education resisted this trend and continued to support the use of Pell Grants in prisons.

But in 1994, Congress took the drastic step of passing a bill making prisoners ineligible for Pell Grants. Overnight, 350 prison education programs closed their doors. The most effective and cost-beneficial correctional policy in the United States collapsed.

A 1997 longitudinal study conducted for the U.S. Department of Education and focusing on three states noted that, "attending school behind bars reduces the likelihood of reincarceration by 29 percent. Translated into savings, every dollar spent on education returned more than two dollars to the citizens in reduced prison costs."

Most strikingly, Texas reported the extraordinary recidivism impacts of postsecondary education: "Two years after release, the overall recidivism rate for college degree holders was as low as 12 percent, and inversely differentiated by type of degree."

If the government got smart and resumed its policy of awarding a small fraction of Pell Grants to qualified incarcerated Americans, Karpowitz and Kenner write, recidivism rates would be cut sharply and millions of dollars saved.

Toward the end of his second term, President Obama did create a program to provisionally offer Pell Grants again at certain institutions. Warden Jim McKinney applied for this when he was a warden at Rockwell City, Iowa, and twenty students there attended night classes as part of the program. The hope was that the program could expand, although it's uncertain what will happen under President Trump. Oakdale administrators did not apply for Pell Grant waivers at the time, and McKinney wasn't yet there to do so.

EIGHTEEN

Instrument of Peace

THE WEEK TRICKLES BY, honey off a spoon. Or maybe it rockets by, runaway bullet train. Whichever subjective mode choir members experience time's passage in, another concert day steals upon us all.

This time the audience will be coming in from outside the walls: community folks, family of insiders, and university dignitaries. Also invited are guests who might be able to help inmates once they're released, through offers of jobs or housing. The idea is to encourage attendees to become aware of the challenges parolees face. And the crowd will be much, much larger. With the concert for inmates, we usually get 20 or 30 men. This community concert will draw more than 200 people.

We gather again in the gymnasium. Before the concert begins, Mary steps onto the podium and we jump into tying up some last-minute loose ends. But things seem a little ragged. Even though last week's concert went well, we're nervous about this one, maybe because of the size of the audience, and the number of dignitaries who will be among them. Among the tenors, a few unanswered questions linger—how much of a piano intro is there before we come in on the first song? When do we shift sections to mixed formation? It puts us a bit on edge.

The guests begin to filter in. They mingle, check out the insider art exhibit on the gym's walls, and then settle into their seats and peruse the program.

Although we feel a bit unprepared, once the concert begins, something happens. Roland repeats the first stanza in his duet with Karletta, throwing her into a panic, but she quickly recovers and their soothing, soaring voices have a galvanizing effect on both choir and audience. I close my eyes as Roland sings. His voice is magnificent.

There's extra instrumentation, too, a trumpet playing on several of the numbers, with beautiful, soaring blasts of sound.

So, despite a few initial missteps, we soon find our groove, after which we're able to relax into the performance. I look down the line at my fellow tenors, fifteen or so men. Dylan smiles back at me. So does Terence.

Now music student Rose steps onto the podium. She shares an anecdote about arranging a version of her father's favorite hymn, "Let There Be Peace on Earth."

"I presented the written arrangement to my father for Christmas last year, along with a box of Twizzlers. He took a look at the sheet music and said, 'Thank you,' without much enthusiasm. Then, he opened the box, and lit up. 'Twizzlers!'"

The audience laughs.

"I wanted him to hear this piece in the flesh," Rose continues, "and feel the excitement of a live performance of it. He's in the audience tonight." She beams, and the song shines.

Occasionally during concerts, insiders are asked to speak about aspects of their lives. An older white insider, Michael, now approaches the mic to talk about AVP. "AVP stands for the Alternatives to Violence Project. You can actually change that to other things, like 'always value people.' It started in 1975 in the New York prison system. It was brought in by Quakers, who helped people deal with their situations in prison in a more non-argumentative way, I guess."

"It came here to Oakdale in 2009, and when it first got here I didn't even pay attention because I didn't think I was a violent person. But after several years of being here, some violence started happening in my brain. So I thought maybe I better take a look at this program and see if it could help me. And after the first class I was hooked. I'm now a facilitator for the program."

Paul strolls to the mic, too, his long hair bouncing off his back, to chip in his two cents worth. Usually ready with a quip, he is serious now. "I started with the AVP program after I found out I did have violence in my life, and it was hard to deal with. I found there were alternatives, that you can actually work out problems without using violence. It has greatly changed my life, because this is a place where violence can happen just like that." He snaps his fingers.

And Bella, university student from England, steps forward to share her volunteer perspective. "Hello," she says, and the audience warms to her accent. "I'm glad that my curiosity kicked in. AVP has shown me that violence comes in a lot of different forms, it could be an eye roll, or a tone of voice, or an action you don't do. The workshop is all about looking inside yourself and learning to make positive choices for the future despite what has happened in the past."

The audience applauds. While the speakers have been speaking, the rest of us have been paging through our folders to find the next song. Now Amy moves to the mic. "The lyrics of our next piece, "Prayer of St. Francis," have particular significance to me now, as I try to help my mother stay comfortable after her stroke six months ago. And even more devastatingly to me, giving as much support as I can to my brother-in-law, as our family tries to come to grips with his recent cancer prognosis."

"I have to say, when I saw some of the songs we'd be singing in the choir, including 'St. Francis,' songs that seemed overtly Christian and religious, I wasn't sure that I'd feel comfortable with the text. But after a couple of rehearsals, I realized that the music and the text and the emotional content of the pieces did resonate with me."

Her voice picks up energy. "Who wouldn't want to be an instrument of peace? Who wouldn't want to console someone in pain? Who wouldn't want to choose actions that could positively influence others? I particularly love the bass, tenor and alto en masse toward the end of the piece, the elegant way the notes flow down the scale in a kind of meditative and quiet natural ceiling of the singers' wish for a vast and generous spirit. The music and lyrics help keep me focused on my intentions, and remind me not to dwell on an uncertain future over which we really have no control."

She returns to her seat and Mary brings us in. The sections—tenor, soprano, alto and bass—start out sharing the melody, but soon break into soaring four-part harmony. It's beautiful.

Where there is hatred, let me bring love, where there is injury, help me to pardon. Where there is doubt, let me bring faith.

When it's over, the audience responds with warm applause.

And now Armand steps up and introduces his composition, "So Much More." With some fervor he talks about how we all need grace. He's good in this role (his father, I've heard, is a preacher). As Karl begins to pound out soulful gospel chords on the piano, Armand launches into a hip-hop cadence.

I am so much more than this charge on my conviction,
I am so much more than all your negative predictions.

His voice is galvanizing, dropping the lyrics with true hip-hop conviction. When we come to the chorus, Armand steps back from the mic, flashes us a glance, and shouts, "Sing it, choir!"

(And the choir sings) *SO MUCH MORE, SO MUCH MORE.*

A revival intensity kicks in and we begin to sway back and forth. The song's lyrics, gospel stylings, and beat are all moving, as is Armand's passionate delivery:

He is so much more than we can ask or imagine, He is so much more
than our minds can fathom.
SO MUCH MORE, SO MUCH MORE.
You are so much more than a victim of rape
You are so much more than a random sex mate
You are so much more than your thoughts of being defeated.
You are so much more than a child that's mistreated
You are so much more than the label of a thug
You are so much more than your addiction to drugs
You are so much more than the late night cries
You are so much more than your thoughts of suicide.
You are so much more than just a human they dog,
When I see you, I see a child of God.

As we reach the end of the song, there's a pregnant moment of silence, the audience letting the power of the music, the pointed message, wash over them. Armand pauses, realizing he's hit a home run. You almost expect him to throw the mic down in triumph. He turns and smiles at his fellow choir members, then salutes us and returns to his seat.

The crowd jumps to its feet, erupting in applause. And from then on, we can do no wrong. With each song, a feeling of collective triumph grows. We let it rip with "Sittin' on the Dock of the Bay." We wow everyone with "Breathe Holy Breath."

The concert wraps up with "May You Walk in Beauty," and we're feeling the love. The audience is effusive in their applause, and in the appreciation they express on the receiving line a few minutes later. Choir members mingle, shaking hands, chatting with community members. Some of the insiders have family in the audience, and they embrace, shedding tears.

I see some friends and wander over to say hello. Everyone is giddy with gratitude.

Many of these audience members have attended several of our concerts, and they seem to agree that this has been one of our better ones. A few of them email comments to Mary Cohen, who shares some with us during rehearsal the following week:

"I can honestly say that the concert was one of the most beautiful and emotional events I've had the privilege of seeing live in person. I was tearing up from the heartfelt commentary in between songs and, of course, the original songs written by inmates."

"I came into the experience not knowing what to expect, and I was truly in awe within the first few minutes. On reflection, I realize I didn't expect to find such honest beauty in a place like that… and it was a gift to be shown how unaware I was."

And, *"We've lived in Iowa City for nearly 20 years and had never really given the prison a second look as we drove by on many occasions. Now, having seen the prisoners and heard them sing and express their thoughts, we have, I believe, a different perspective on the place and the people inside. The concert was definitely eye-opening. I don't know what they did to get there, and I'm not sure it matters. I hope the experience with the choir helps them do their time and become productive citizens when they are released."*

"I think your efforts are to be lauded. As we move to a privatized prison system in this country, with its focus on profits and cost containment, rather than ostensibly rehabilitation, I wonder if there will be any place for programs like yours. I certainly hope so."

At the end of rehearsal, Tyrone stands and addresses the outside singers.

"I want you to know that choir is a shining high point of our week. When I leave rehearsal, I go back to my cell, all hyped up, and my cellmates are like—'What's with you?' We just appreciate you guys so much."

WINTER BREAK

NINETEEN

All On This Train Ride Together

THE SEASON WANES, A crescendo of sound supplanted by sudden silence, as we ease into the depths of winter. The choir will not meet for six weeks around the holidays, and the break gives me time to reflect on my experience, read more about prison issues, and speak with other people who are working in the field of restorative justice.

I'm headed east to visit some friends. A festive atmosphere reigns in my Amtrak compartment, as people ride the rails home for holiday reunions with loved ones. Passengers chat easily with strangers about their destinations, and as evening falls, faces staring out at the passing countryside are reflected back into the car in the darkening windows.

At the next station stop, a man enters our compartment, lugging an impossibly large and heavy suitcase down the aisle. He sits behind me, muttering. There's something a little odd about him.

For one thing, his concept of fitting in to this little community on the train seems skewed. He shouts into his phone late at night when people are trying to sleep. Emotion fills his voice. When someone across the aisle asks him to keep his voice down, he gets defensive. He says, "You take care of yourself, and don't worry about me."

"I bought a ticket," he huffs, as if that entitles him to do what he will on the train. He's ready to come to blows.

A pall of discomfort settles over the passengers in our section of the car. *Why can't we all just get along?*

In the dim light, I get to thinking. About how actions can be like ripples circling out from a stone tossed into a pool. About behaviors that become ingrained, sometimes because of trauma. Or sometimes because of pure selfishness. I think about some of the guys in the choir I've gotten to know, and how their lives became ensnared in tumbling domino patterns of events.

The man sitting behind me appears to have limited self-awareness. But then I remember how I've reacted when I've been in a situation that stressed me. For example, speeding down the interstate, late and in a rush to get somewhere, when someone cuts me off, and suddenly, in spite of all my intentions to be a reflective person, I'm caught up in a moment of reactive anger, ready to overtake that driver and put him in his place.

"Idiot," I find myself fuming under my breath. I wonder if it's the anonymity of the road that raises these feelings. I have no context for understanding other drivers, don't know their lives, and thus cut them less slack.

The rough truth is, we all transgress. We commit blunders, lose our cool, and I'd go so far as to say that we all commit crimes, in one way or another, at one time or another. Of course, some crimes are more serious than others. Still, "the jury, passing on the prisoner's life," Shakespeare reminds us, "may in the sworn twelve have a thief or two guiltier than him they try."

Whether they're religious commandments, the penal code, drug laws, or rules of the road, at some time in our lives we break the rules society has set up to maintain order. And for many of us, when we realize that we've screwed up, that we've stepped into a place of shame and possible humiliation, I think, deep down, that we hope for understanding from those around us.

I appreciate the metaphor of society as a group of pilgrims traveling together in a caravan.[67] If any of these travelers falls behind, or stumbles, or becomes ill, the group steps up and accommodates them, helping this person along the way. They don't leave anyone behind. It's about forward, collective movement. If we were to actually apply this prescription to society as a whole, including the incarcerated, how would it change things?

In *Tattoos on the Heart*, Greg Boyle writes about working with gang members in Los Angeles. He started a business called Home Boy Industries to give jobs to ex-gangbangers. His book reveals the deep need in many of these gang members to feel loved and respected, and their desire to turn away from crime when offered these qualities in another setting. Reflecting on his approach, Boyle says, "We imagine a circle of compassion. Then we imagine no one standing outside that circle, moving ourselves closer to the margins so that the margins themselves will be erased. We stand there with those whose dignity has been denied."[68]

This reminds me of a meditation practice called *metta* (a meditation, interestingly, that Mary Cohen will lead the choir in at one point). It goes like this: closing your eyes, you think about and expand your sense of love, your compassion, to those you know and like. Then you move on to those you don't know, someone you might pass in the hallway or on the street. And then you focus on those you may dislike.

It can be a surprising exercise, conjuring into awareness the presence and struggles of people you may not usually think about, and forging connections with them.

What's the saying? Be kind, for everyone you meet is fighting a great battle.

I would never argue that there aren't crimes that are not extremely harmful to society, or that there aren't people in or out of prison who don't pose an ongoing danger.

But just as focusing on individual lines on a canvas doesn't reveal the big picture and it's only when you step back and take in the painting as a whole that your perspective shifts, so a complicated constellation of factors weaves through these stories of criminal justice, factors that are important to understand. The growth and utility of prisons is not removed from what's happening in any individual city, or the country, at large.

I live in a neighborhood with several low-income apartment complexes. There's some hunger and homelessness (a homeless man was retiring at night into the utility closet of one apartment building on cold winter nights, unbeknownst to anyone, until he started a fire with a smoldering cigarette). The housing crisis that came to a head after the mortgage scandal of 2008 lingers on. There seem to be a greater number of ambulance calls to this neighborhood, as well as more police visits, at least anecdotally. What this suggests is that poverty is not good for one's health, and that unemployment can lead people to make bad choices.

It's not always easy to find a job with good wages in this region. Many Iowa counties' wages remain stagnant. The schools are good here, though the question of parity between schools in richer and poorer parts of our community dogs us. But the Iowa legislature, currently dominated by conservative legislators, continues to reduce funding for public education, and especially in rural counties, the schools are struggling. In other parts of the country, things are worse. Down the road in St. Louis, a friend who taught in the school system confirms that many mostly African American schools inside the great ring road of the city or across the Mississippi in East St. Louis are floundering.

Some of these problems come down to the great disparity our society has cultivated in the inequality of income. And a lot of that, I believe, comes down to the shameful logic of capitalism. Take the matter of CEO compensation. The average ratio of CEO to worker wages in the U.S. is a mind-blowing 360 to 1. In Canada it's 20 to 1, and in Germany 12 to 1.[69] The shift to deregulation in recent decades has seen half of American corporations sending jobs overseas, resulting in hundreds of thousands of jobs lost in the U.S. Outsourcing also drives down wages and benefits.

We've allowed a system to flourish based on wringing maximum profit out of workers, consumers and the environment, often at the expense of a sense of cooperation, community building, and our own health and wealth. For example, despite their principal role in causing the 2008 Great Recession, Wall Street financial institutions—whose *raison d'etre*, let's face it, is simply to make money off of money—are expanding, unregulated, more than ever before. Meanwhile, those in the highest political office model the selfish behavior that sets the tone for this expansion.

What does this all mean? Mark Lewis Taylor suggests that these issues of wealth and class create "social wreckage" that "has to be managed, cleaned up or dispensed with. This makes up the surplus populations that our economic system has to manage and that the U.S. controls today to a growing extent by systems of punishment and confinement." [70]Our prisons are full of poor people.

While individuals must take responsibility for what they do, there are social factors that shape people's lives, communities and decisions. And perhaps it's only when we embrace a transformative and restorative view of society as a whole, that we'll be able to realize true justice in our justice system.

We're all connected, and the way we treat each other, the conditions we allow to flourish, outside of prison and in, reflect the quality of that connection. We're all on this train ride together.

TWENTY

Jim Crow Redux

EACH SEASON, THREE OR four African American, and several Latino men sing in the choir. There are, of course, many more people of color than that in the prison, but for whatever reason—maybe the kind of music we sing doesn't appeal to them—only a few join.

Iowa is as white a state as they come, but the numbers of black and brown people in prison here stand greatly out of proportion to their numbers as a whole. African Americans in Iowa are arrested and jailed at around eight times the rate of people of other races. It's an infuriating figure. Blacks make up three percent of the overall Iowa population, but they're 23 percent of the Iowa prison population. In the U.S. as a whole, those figures are 12 percent of the total population and 37 percent of inmates.

When, I wonder, did we become a nation, and a state, that locked up its poor people of color? That's sort of a trick question. The answer is, we've always done so. Take a look at U.S. history, at how this country was built—slavery, economic imperialism, exploitation of poor immigrant working people, violation of treaties, institutional and general racism—and you'll understand what I mean.

For African Americans these days, the criminal justice system serves as a gateway into a larger system of permanent marginalization. That's the argument legal scholar Michelle Alexander has made in her book *The New Jim Crow: Mass Incarceration in the Age of Colorblindness*. Our contemporary justice system, Alexander claims, rivals Jim Crow, the post-Civil War system of laws designed to hold black people back, which gave rise to a period marked by lynching and other forms of violence against blacks.

African Americans are no more likely to use or sell drugs than whites, but they're made criminals at much higher rates for doing so. White students use cocaine at seven times the rate of black students. White young people are a third more likely to have sold drugs than black ones, and yet, black incarceration for drug offenses is six times higher in Iowa.[71]

Some of this can be traced to the origins of the explosion in the U.S. prison population. In the mid-'80s, predominantly black inner city communities suffered economic collapse. Crack hit the streets, easier to sell than cocaine, and became the drug of choice in many cities. Prior to '86, the longest sentence for drug possession was one year. President Reagan pushed for the Anti-Drug Abuse Act of 1986, which laid out mandatory minimum sentences, and a more severe punishment for crack than cocaine.[72]

Reagan convinced law enforcement that this war should be a priority. He awarded cash to police departments, in the form of the so-called 'Byrne grants.' SWAT raids increased. Police departments were allowed to keep the assets they seized, increasing the size of their budget. There was pressure to keep arrest numbers up. Alexander suggests black neighborhoods faced police practices that would provoke widespread outrage if they were committed in white, middle-class areas.

Yet defendants were typically denied proper representation, pressured to plea bargain, and often pled guilty to crimes they didn't commit for fear of mandatory sentences. Most arrests are not for dealing, or for dangerous drugs—simple possession of marijuana made up 80 percent of arrests in the '90s.[73]

All of this is happening, of course, in the context of ongoing police brutality toward people of color. The spate of police shootings of black men is nothing new; it's only coming to the fore because cell phone technology has made it much easier to publicize such incidents. As a white man, I breeze through my days exercising the gifts of white privilege and inoculation from police violence. I can't really understand what it's like to face that kind of culture-wide pressure. But at the very least, I can give a damn.

It's a failure to care that lies at the core of this system. Rather than shaming and condemning an already deeply stigmatized group—the incarcerated—Alexander suggests we instead collectively embrace them; not their behavior, but their humanness. We could talk about race, not be color-blind. We could deal with structural racism through job creation, educational reform, and restorative justice programs.

We could, Alexander suggests, choose to be a nation that extends care and compassion to those who are locked up and locked out; we could treat them like one of 'us.'

A year in prison slips by at a pace that depends on the perceptions of the individual, my insider friends tell me. Some things seem eternal; others are ephemeral. There's the passing of the seasons, mostly viewed through a window. There are visits from family. The annual review/parole board meeting. Apart from that, it's all about what makes you tick, what you're interested in, what can either help you to stand outside of time in a way that massages its painful passage, or help you purposefully embrace time, moving into a more meaningful relationship with it.

Keith's year revolved around sports on TV and a few other highlights. He watched football in the fall, then hockey, his annual review was around December, then came Christmas, his birthday in April, and the NCAA Softball World Series in June. Then he waited for football to start up again.

On a day-to-day level, every day was pretty much the same, a simple, repetitive, routine. After breakfast he would go to work, running inmates. Then there was head count. More work. Another count. He might go to the yard for some exercise. After dinner, he watched TV, read, wrote some letters, went back to his cell and went to sleep.

Of course, permeating his daily routine like groundwater seeping into a well was a longing for the things he sorely missed: Family and friends. Playing hockey. Cooking. Things most people take for granted, like driving a car, going to a coffee shop, or working in a kitchen. He missed attending baseball games. He missed flirting. When he'd worked in the restaurant, he'd always flirted with the waitresses. It was hard not to do this in the choir. He had to remind himself not to flirt.

In some ways, he'd been lucky. So far, he'd received no major disciplinary actions, though he didn't always see eye to eye with policy, procedure, or staff.

One time, for example, he forgot his ID in his cell. A CO berated him and threatened to write him up. Some people, he sensed, felt they needed to punish you just for being in prison.

My thermostat on prison issues continues to ratchet up. After finishing Michelle Alexander's book, I move on to other books lying on my bedside table. These include Elizabeth Hinton's "From the War on Poverty to the War on Crime: The Making of Mass Incarceration in America," and Laura Edge's "Locked Up: A History of the US Prison System." And as I research the history of American prisons, one thing stands out: the changeability of public perceptions—the old pendulum swing—over time about crime and punishment.

Early in the twentieth century, many efforts to improve the penal system took place. These were interspersed with cycles of reaction and clampdown. And it's continued like that up to the present day.

The Progressive Era (1900-1920) saw the growth of reforms such as probation and parole, as well as indeterminate sentences, which gave judges some discretion.

The archetypal striped uniforms—visual symbols of scourging and the lash—were discontinued. Prisons became cleaner, better organized, and offered more activities. But as Laura Edge notes, the high ideals of the Progressive Era fell short: "Criminals were not 'cured' and crime was not eliminated." [74]

During this period, there were also attempts to legislate morality. The Mann Act of 1910 (which targeted prostitution), the Narcotic Act of 1914, and Prohibition beginning in 1920 were all efforts by legislators to force people to become good. We know how some of that turned out. The prohibition experiment, while shining a spotlight on the widespread ills of public drunkenness, yielded wildly uneven results. Though it did cut consumption in half, criminal gangs took control of the liquor supply, creating a huge black economy for booze.

Several states allowed the forced sterilization of criminals, which they thought would prevent the passing on of "defective genes" to children. In 1942 the Supreme Court ruled against this practice, based on the Constitution's Equal Protection Clause.

Prisons became even more overcrowded during the uncertainty and despair of the Great Depression, and there was an increase in prison riots. Former attorney general George Wickersham chaired a national panel in 1931 that argued that prisons themselves were contributing to the increase of crime by hardening the prisoner.

During World War II, prison populations dropped. Many inmates—the majority of those who were eligible and had not been convicted of serious crimes—were drafted and placed under the Army's control. Those who remained inside often contributed to the war effort by donating blood, volunteering to take part in malaria research, and manufacturing supplies such as shoes, shirts, blankets and bunks.

Leap forward to the 1950s, and the buzzword "correction" gains currency. A medical and psychological model of criminology was coming to the fore. The American Prison Association changed its name to the American Correctional Association. Criminals committed crimes, the theory went, because of psychological problems, and they needed to be treated, rather than punished.

Guards were now to be called correctional officers, more psychologists were employed, and vocational training programs were implemented. It was all about professionalization and a scientific approach, including the growth of diagnostic centers, treatment programs, and behavioral modification. Prisons offered new classes to inmates in subjects ranging from commercial art to typing, and provided more athletic programs, libraries and gyms.

In the 1960s, much like life outside of prisons, human rights became a primary concern, including the Miranda rights of the arrested, and the constitutional rights of prisoners. Inmates could, for the first time, write letters to people on the outside. Prison guards were forced to stop all forms of corporal punishment, based on the Eighth Amendment. Prisoners were allowed to file lawsuits and appeals.

It was during this period that community corrections programs first developed, and began to prepare inmates for life after prison. These included work-release programs and halfway houses, which helped ex-convicts find jobs, and provided room and board, counseling and recreation.

In 1968, for the first time in U.S. history, there were no state-sanctioned killings, reflecting a general sentiment in the country that capital punishment was inhumane. In 1972, the Supreme Court ruled that the death penalty constituted cruel and unusual punishment, violating the 8th and 14th Amendments, because African Americans, the poor and other disadvantaged groups were executed more often than other groups. Almost immediately, states began to write their own death penalty laws. (And in 1976 the Supreme Court declared the death penalty constitutional again).

The '60s had seen the single largest reduction ever in prison populations. When Nixon was elected, though, he began to build prisons at an unprecedented rate. Raids, wiretapping, and mandatory minimum sentences increased. Local crimes like drug dealing and gambling became federal offenses. SWAT teams were formed to raid Black Panther headquarters.

The RICO act allowed federal agents to interrogate anyone, anywhere, for any reason.[75]

By the mid-'70s only 10 percent of the billions spent on corrections went to rehabilitation, and prison populations surged. A get-tough attitude on crime surfaced in the '70s and '80s, which gave rise to fixed-length or determinate sentences, and later, to the three strikes law, starting in California in the '90s.

According to Robert Perkinson, both presidents Reagan and the first Bush built a punitive legacy; under their watch, the federal prison population doubled, mostly due to drug crimes. [76]On the heels of this, President Clinton announced that in order to qualify for federal support, states had to increase their prison budgets, and cut back on sentence reductions for good time and parole.

It was Democrat Clinton, with the Omnibus Crime Bill of 1994, who presided over the most intensive incarceration boom in U.S. history.

I have a friend who's teaching a bridge class. He's been down for 46 years, turned down for parole twice. He's started to doubt he'll ever leave. One can see what it costs him in his face and his posture.

— Henry

TWENTY-ONE

The Accountability Part

ONE WINTER NIGHT IN 1980, a few friends and I were parked on an undeveloped cul-de-sac on the edge of our Texas town, finishing off a case of Lone Star beer, when the spinning blue and white lights of a police cruiser rolled up behind our car, freeze-framing us in drunken panic. A cop got out and approached us.

Playing his flashlight beam over the car's interior and spotting the beer, he asked us to roll down our windows. Sizing up the situation and sighing, he got into instructive mode, sharing with us the story of how he was recently called to the scene of an accident. A car had smashed into an embankment, and the teenaged occupants, who had been drinking, were found dead. After telling us this story, he let us go with a warning, perhaps because we were white.

Was I moved by this 'scared straight' story? Not so much. In those days, as I've noted, I was pulled in conflicting directions, the Saturday night-Sunday morning split. Faith, respectability, values my parents tried to instill in me, on one hand. On the other, and perhaps in that moment more important—the approval of my friends, a need to feel wild and free, and a gap in my own self-understanding, which I attempted to plug with drugs and alcohol.

On another afternoon, though no beer was involved, I plowed my parents' Corolla into the back of another car simply because I wasn't paying proper attention to the road, but was off in my own world. No one was hurt, thank goodness, and there were no real consequences apart from my having to pay to have the car repaired.

I was, I have to admit, in a dark place in that period of my life. One of the questions I faced, perhaps inchoately, was how to shine a light of self-mastery and awareness into that darkness, without riding a road to self-destruction, or breaking what didn't deserve to be broken.

Had the cards of fate fallen slightly differently in those sultry Texas days, my life might have taken a very peculiar twist. Forget about speeding tickets; my friends and I indulged in various drugs frequently enough that the chance of arrest for possession was not totally outside the realm of possibility. And if I had, by some cruel stroke, gone to jail (though my background and upbringing would probably have worked to my advantage), what might I have felt?

Putting myself into those shoes isn't easy. I imagine I would have experienced tremendous shame and confusion, grief, an abundance of anger, and a sense of regret. In short, a powerful brew of turbulent emotions compounding the emotional morass I already was slogging through as a young man.

Nothing like that happened, of course. My point is that my energies needed redirecting.

Some traditional societies cultivate a ritualized method for initiating and leading young people from the difficulties of adolescence into the responsibilities of adulthood. What if mainstream American culture offered more skillful elder-led ceremonies for adolescents to understand and take their place in the world?

I've heard of one community elder who leads rituals for gang members. He tells them to bring a stone for everyone they've lost to gang violence and place it in a pile. Invariably, the pile of stones mounts. There's so much grief there. But the ritualization of the grief helps to contain and express it.

It doesn't have to be structured. Reaching out to young people, offering advice and companionship, is something most of us can do.

I could certainly have benefitted from more adult guidance as a teenager. I made plenty of mistakes. But somehow, with the passage into my early 20s, the help of some mentors, and a sense of structure in the spiritual tradition I was embracing, I was able to learn from those mistakes and forge a more stable, responsible identity. I'm still learning, of course.

Mistakes, bad choices, often rooted in a lack of self-understanding, a sense of selfishness, or a sense of despair, are what landed many of the guys at Oakdale. Certainly, everyone has to take responsibility for his or her own actions. (And I am sensitive to victims' criticisms of describing crimes as simply 'mistakes'). The question is, do people receive the opportunity to learn from their wrong actions and chart a new course?

'I never realized the depth of the harm I caused.'

Mary Roche has heard this a lot from insiders. As director of the Office of Victim Services and Restorative Justice for the state of Iowa, she's organized a number of impact programs, which bring crime victims into prisons to share their stories with offenders. Hearing these stories, insiders sometimes experience a 'waking up' moment.

Roche's work includes facilitating letter exchanges between victim and offender, aimed at increasing a sense of accountability. She also oversees a Seeking Safety group for treatment of Post-Traumatic Stress Disorder, helping address symptoms.

Unfortunately, the DOC got rid of the victim impact program. They didn't feel it was evidence-based, and the DOC, Roche says, is all about what returns the biggest bang for their buck. Lack of funding is always an issue. But most of the research the DOC draws on is related to employment, education, and substance abuse, not restorative justice, even though there's a great deal of research on the benefits of this kind of work.

Such work, as I've noted earlier, involves the effort to promote healing between all parties. This includes recognizing that the one who caused harm is also a person.

"That's a really difficult place to get to," Roche says. "Not everyone wants to get there. A lot of victims have no interest in forgiveness, or in ever meeting the offender. They may want punishment. Or the death penalty. I believe, though, that there are more people than not who seek some kind of healing."

Roche comes at this from a very personal place.

Years before becoming director of restorative justice for the state, while she was studying for her master's degree in mental health counseling at the University of Northern Iowa, her husband, Joe, was hit and killed by a drunk driver.

Suddenly, her life was jaggedly, horrifically upended. She desperately tried to process her grief as she contemplated a future without a husband and father for her two-year old son. How to live in a world from which her love had been so tragically wrenched?

Roche feels the system protected the man who killed her husband from understanding the reality of what he'd done. There'd been no trial, only a hearing. There was no context helping him understand the impact of his crime. It was not just, Roche felt. It was not right.

As time passed, she began to feel the need to see and talk to this man, Robert, who was now in prison. To share with him something about whom Joe was. She had questions for him; but mostly she needed a sense of closure.

At the hearing Robert had said he was sorry, that it had been an accident. Roche learned that he was an alcoholic, and wondered what he would do with his feelings of guilt. Maybe, she worried, when he had the opportunity, he would start using again. Maybe he would cause further harm.

Although her request to meet Robert was turned down the first time, the second time she approached the DOC she was given permission. A new victim-offender mediation program had just been put in place.

A mediator helped her prepare for the encounter. But as she entered the prison room, she said it felt like all of the air had been sucked out of the space. Minutes passed before she was even able to look at Robert. More time passed before he could look her in the eye. He was nervous, but he did seem to want to be helpful; he was eager to answer Roche's questions.

And he said the words she wanted to hear: 'I'm responsible for Joe's death.' They began to talk about their lives. His, she learned, had been full of trauma and loss.

One thing Roche wanted was for Robert to understand her husband's journey. Joe had been a recovering alcoholic himself, whom she had met after he became sober. AA had basically saved Joe's life, and he'd gone on to sponsor many people. The irony of Joe being killed by an alcoholic was not lost on Roche. She shared some of the things she'd learned from Joe, and showed him a photo album of their lives. Basically, she shared her pain with him. She bawled through most of it.

And there was another poignant message to share. Roche's son, Sam—age 6 by this time—had recorded an audiotape, which she played for Robert. On the tape, Sam talked about what it was like to grow up without a dad. For one thing, he hadn't learned how to fish. He hadn't learned how to play sports, either. He and his mom had built a jungle gym in their yard, but it took them a lot longer with only Mom to do it.

Finally, Sam worried aloud on the tape, would Robert ever come back and kill someone else in his family?

The process of meeting victim's needs is about acknowledgment and recognition. Victims want the offender to understand the pain they've caused, to see how their lives have been affected. This can be healing. "When Robert left the room," Roche says, "I was left with an overwhelming feeling of gratitude. In my mind I was thinking, you can't say thank you to him. But when I left the room he was still out there, and I called to him. The COs got uptight, but he came over, and I thanked him, and shook his hand."

It was a significant moment for her. It was one thing to talk about her loss with friends; quite another to talk to the man who was the cause of it. The exchange helped release some of her burden.

When you're bent on vengeance, you stay connected to the trauma. It can, in a strange way, keep you connected to the one you love. "I didn't want to stop hurting," Roche says. "The pain made a connection to Joe. To let go of that can feel like another death. Did I really want to feel happiness again?"

"People get stuck. I don't judge them. Let them be where they are. I know a woman whose daughter had been raped and murdered on prom night. We can't imagine the kind of pain that person is in. And usually we don't want to acknowledge it; we want the ugliness to go away. We want the person to hurry up and heal. And so a lot of people are left to find their own way."

Roche's story doesn't end there. Robert was released, and later faced another OWI charge. He appeared before the same judge, and got two more years in prison. Roche thought she'd go see him again.

As per the system, a mediator went in first. The mediator came back and told Roche, "This is the most criminally-thinking person I've met in a long time. He's willing to meet you. But I don't recommend it." Robert had expressed all sorts of rationalizations and crazy stories related to Joe and Mary. One wonders if he'd had a psychological breakdown. It came as a shock, and Roche was distressed.

"But I realized I hadn't let go completely. So I sent a letter to him. 'You don't owe me anything,' I wrote. 'I'm done with you.' I had felt that if Robert would change, it would give Joe's life and death meaning. But I couldn't give Robert the power to determine the meaning of Joe's life."

Clearly, these are complicated matters. Becoming accountable, atoning for one's crimes as a perpetrator, as well as gaining a sense of closure as a victim—such things don't play out in clear, simple lines. Roche had to learn to see things for what they were—flawed and messy. But perhaps it was that messiness that held the key to change. Change sometimes happens in a one-step-forward, two-steps-back fashion. Recovering addicts will often undergo ten or fifteen relapses, over a period of years, before getting completely clean. We never know what the next moment will bring, and sometimes planting a seed is all we can do.

As a restorative justice worker, Roche appreciates programs like the Oakdale Choir. It's an important piece of the puzzle, she says, offering insiders the chance to give something back.

She tells me about a vital exchange which grew out of the choir. In 2010 a sexual abuse survivor named Elma heard about a song penned by an Oakdale Choir insider called "In My Mother's Eyes." Moved, Elma wrote a poem entitled "Inside a Mother's Heart."

Inside a mother's heart, search deep and you will find
The treasures of tomorrow, and the tears she leaves behind.

Mary Cohen learned of Elma's poem, and together with a few inside songwriters she expanded the lyrics and set it to music.

Trade tears for understanding, let patience bring you growth,
Find hope to encourage your spirit, to discover your God-given worth.

The choir sang the song at a summer songwriting workshop concert, and Elma attended. Hearing the song performed, seeing the lines of connection between those involved in creating it, helped her, she says, to realize something: we are all more than the worst thing we've ever done. And she herself was more than a victim.

Restorative justice initiatives often bring victims and their families together with perpetrators and their families. Maya Schenwar says both sides must be willing to meet, and victims are never forced to confront offenders if they don't want to. Members of the community are also invited to observe and offer input. "They all sit in a circle and talk about what happened, what led up to it, and how they were affected. Victims can say what would help them to move on. The perpetrators also tell their side of the story."[77]

The goal is to reach a consensus, led by the victim, on how to make restitution. The process helps both sides see each other as human beings. Schenwar offers a caveat, though, for sexual assault situations: "Very often the victim does not want to be in a room with the perpetrator, even with counseling and after time has passed. We need to prioritize the victims' needs in these situations. We can't use the same model to deal with every offense."

Roche says it's vitally important that the piece about offenders' individual atonement, and being accountable—the connection to the victim—is there. Offenders have to figure out how to make amends in an intentional way: to do something kind, with intention. Or to change their thoughts from "I have taken and taken," to "Now I need to give something."

As Roche speaks, I'm nodding along, telling her that I've realized that prisoners are just like everyone else, that everyone makes mistakes. She stops me.

"It's common for volunteers to say, 'Everyone makes mistakes, everyone sins.' I want to lean in on that accountability part. I like the idea of embracing the offender, and the focus on redemption. But we do a disservice when we don't help these offenders deal with the magnitude of their mistakes. We can't whitewash it. We need to be willing to get down into the mud, and listen. Counselors who say 'I don't want to know the details' won't be able to help them, really."

"Whitewashing allows them to hang on to their bits of shame," she continues. "They may say, 'I've been forgiven. God forgives me.' Well, yay for you. Do you want to know what's going on with your victim?"

"It's not real, really, until you deal with the impact on the victim. If you don't deal with all of that, it *will* affect you."

Point taken.

TWENTY-TWO

Broken Beyond Repair?

"THE VERY MECHANISMS IN the brain that allow adversity to get under the skin are also the mechanisms that enable awakening," says neuroscientist Richard Davidson.[78] Earlier in the book I noted how early traumatic experiences can lead to criminal behavior, as per Paul Renn's research. But there is also a lot of up-and-coming research about how it's never too late to reprogram the brain. How the brain's 'neuroplasticity' allows for changes in behavior at any age. How what we practice, we become. This holds tremendous potential for people with addictions, and for people with criminal tendencies.

I've talked about this a bit with Sally Schwager. A Connecticut therapist, Schwager started volunteering a few years ago with the Osborne Association, an organization that offers a 12-week training in restorative justice counseling. She was interested in working on something called the "Long-Termers Responsibility Project." This program was designed to help inmates convicted of murder and saddled with a long-term sentence work toward atonement. The association vetted each inside individual with a particular end in mind: were they open to expressing remorse? And were they willing to take responsibility for their actions?

The more I explore prison issues, the more dynamic, caring people active in prison work I encounter. I met Sally when I did some coursework in spiritual counseling through another institute in New York, where she was one of the directors. In one of the classes I took with her she talked about these issues of neuroplasticity and reprogramming the brain. Because she has also worked with people convicted of violent offenses and sentenced to long terms, I asked her to share with me what she had learned. Would ideas of restorative justice work with these so-called hardened, violent, criminals?

Any act of violence has a ripple effect, Schwager says. It affects the victim, the family, the offender him or herself, and the community in which the violence takes place. Putting together a team to work with each inmate, the Responsibility Project looks at the impact of this violence from many angles.

Schwager has worked with several incarcerated people in New York, especially at Fishkill Correctional Facility in Beacon, including a 30-year old woman who went to prison at the age of 15, and a man who shot a taxi driver.

When she began working with a third person, a man named Alex, he'd been in prison for 27 years. Alex would be going up before his sixth parole board soon.

The truth is, his crime was horrendous. He'd decided to rob someone, and asked himself, 'Who can I rob that doesn't matter? Who's the lowest of the low? Who wouldn't go to the police?' The answer he came up with was a hooker. This reflected his fundamental view of women.

Alex engaged a prostitute, and they drove to an isolated area and had oral sex. He was driving her back, but he began going in the wrong direction, planning to rob her, and she started fighting back. Trying to subdue her, Alex strangled and killed her.

He left the woman in a deserted lot, covered with garbage, and set her body on fire. It was revealed at trial that the woman had been pregnant. Alex received a sentence of 20 years to life.

In prison, Schwager has learned, everyone claims, 'I didn't do it.' A lawyer tries to shape a defendant's story, and tries to minimize the impact of the violence. No one talks about their crime. Everyone's innocent. For decades, Alex didn't talk about or lied about his crime. Part of this was pure self-preservation—in the prison hierarchy, those who harm babies are considered the lowest.

Over the years, Alex has had to work through his shame in order to talk about what happened. Schwager's work included trying to help Alex feel what it must have been like for his victim, to identify and empathize with her life and her pain. He needed to learn how to feel compassion for this woman.

For decades, the woman whom Alex killed had no name. She was buried in a potters' field, on a little island in the Hudson River. Schwager showed a picture of the site to Alex. In an effort to humanize her, Alex eventually gave the woman a name—Lisa. They talked about what she had looked like that night, what she had said. It was about trying to call her into the room. Every time a new piece of the puzzle was unveiled, Alex's heart softened.

They learned of a woman who'd been the victim of a similar crime and Schwager brought this woman's sister in to meet Alex. It was an intense encounter. Warily, the murderer and the family member eyed each other, then, slowly, told each other their stories. In the end, Schwager says, it was very healing for both of them. The woman wept to hear Alex's remorse. Alex sobbed to hear her story, and at the realization that she was in so much pain. They cried together.

And this, partly, is what the program aims for—helping insiders feel what the other person feels. Remorse equals empathy.

And then, in a second phase, Alex also needed to begin to feel compassion for himself. He had to discover his own wholeness, in order to heal the brokenness that had contributed to the mindset that led to his crime.

To do this, they looked at his past.

An offender's childhood is often as bad as anything you can imagine, Schwager says. To commit violence, you have to be numb. The guy who killed the cabbie, for example, had been constantly beaten up at school. When he was six, he was chased home from school by other kids. "He ran to his mother, who was standing outside, to that source of unconditional safety, right? She slapped him and pushed him back to fight. That day he beat the other kids to a pulp. He did that to earn his mother's love."

Alex had an abusive father, who beat his mother, Alex, and the other siblings. His father made him kneel on grains of uncooked rice for long periods of time, a bizarre but painful punishment. Alex would go numb and freeze, not knowing what to do. This sense of numbness would pop up again throughout his life whenever he was faced with overwhelming circumstances.

One of the questions I've been grappling with comes up in my conversation with Schwager. The question is this: Can someone be broken beyond repair? Can a person lose their sense of empathy completely?

She pauses. "If I believed that," she says, "it would be hard to do this work. Although some people working on this project do feel there is a brokenness beyond which someone can't come back."

Schwager says Alex opens and softens but she's not always sure that it sticks. He can be an opportunist, sometimes. But other times she looks at him and thinks, "There is a transformed man. He has done a lot of work." She would trust him to babysit her son if he were released, she says.

A growing sense of responsibility begins to take shape for some of these people, a shift in attitude reflecting the idea of neuroplasticity. Schwager led the man who killed the cab driver in an exercise. She put him into the shoes of the man's family. He felt deeply for the cabbie's daughters and grandchildren. The man ended up writing a heartfelt letter to the community of taxi drivers in New York City, apologizing for the terror he had caused.

Of course, in prison, it's not always safe to allow oneself to be so vulnerable. Schwager helps the people she's working with to open themselves, to breathe and feel how it is to be in their hearts, but then also to ground themselves so they can go back to their cell and cope with other inmates.

Every two years the long-termers go before the parole board. They have seven minutes with the board on an interactive video feed. Seven minutes to show that they've been rehabilitated, to demonstrate that they deserve to be out.

Many parole commissioners are ex-cops whose bias against murderers is well-known. If someone has murdered, they don't want to let him out of prison. Schwager says the 'energetics' of the inmate, their sense of presence, is important. They need to authentically show they've done deep work, that they feel empathy. They have to energetically show up. The work is intense in the weeks before the board hearing.

The parole board will try to trigger the anger or shame of the inmate, push their buttons, to see if they've dealt with their issues. Taking responsibility through their language is important. Not, 'The gun went off,' but 'I pulled the trigger.'

As for the first inmate Schwager worked with, the woman, her last appearance before the board was remarkable. She said, "No one has the power to imprison me anymore. I'm liberated by this work." The board could see the change in her. And she was paroled.

Sometimes the most difficult people in jail, Schwager feels, are the officers. There was a CO who was actually named Officer Rough. He would call out in a sing-song voice when Schwager arrived, "I'm ready for some re-hab-ili-ta-tion!" Another time he asked her, "What are you doing here with these scumbags?"

Schwager refrained from responding to this kind of provocation, understanding that antagonizing the staff could affect the program.

The work, though, has dispelled a lot of stereotypes for her. "I always felt very different from people in prison," she says. "They were the 'other.' Especially murderers. Now I look for ways in which we're not different."

Ultimately, it's up to the individual how they do their time, she says. "You can become a lawyer or you can become a drug addict."

"I love and admire Alex a lot. And through this work I have looked at my own capacity for violence. It's a real process to stay in my heart."

There are small signs of change. One man had been on my radar for a while; he had a white power slogan tattooed on his forearm. One day, out of the blue, he told me he wanted to do some research on creams that can erase tattoos.

— *Warden Jim McKinney*

SPRING

TWENTY-THREE

Shattering Stereotypes

HEAVY SNOW BLANKETS EASTERN Iowa. Trudging through the frigid parking lot from my car to the prison entrance, I hear an unmistakable sound and glance up at the sky. A flock of geese is passing overhead, several long trailing 'V' contingents, punctuating the frozen air with their loud, lovely honks. A few moments later a single goose, separated, speeds across the sky in search of his tribe.

February has rolled around, and it's time for the choir to start up again. I haven't rubbed elbows with my choir compatriots for six weeks; I'm looking forward to it. I marvel at how being in the OCC has come to imprint the seasons, serving as an emotional and musical anchor for fall and spring.

Turning the corner from the prison corridor and entering the rehearsal space, familiar faces pop throughout the room. I walk over and shake hands with Chip.

"How are you?"

"OK, all things considered."

I take a seat next to a talkative and charming insider named Dylan, whom I always enjoy interacting with. He tells me he's learning Chinese, studying phrases from books in the library.

The energy in the room seems a little different. Several people remark on it. It's as if, after several years in existence, the choir is coming into its own. Our musicianship seems stronger, our harmonizing tighter.

As an icebreaker this first rehearsal back, Mary asks us to meet someone we don't know and tell them three things: your name, how long you've been in the choir, and a memory of a previous choir experience. I make eye contact with Reggie, a white man of about sixty with a full beard and a belly. He often accompanies the choir on guitar. We stand to the side and introduce ourselves. I tell him how I have always enjoyed hearing Burt's high tenor on "Walk in Beauty" soaring above the group.

He laughs. "Burt's one of my roommates," he says. "And we sing in the church choir together, which I direct. He's a great guy. In the cell, he'll say something like, 'Now how did I get all these candy bars?' and throw them to the other cellmates."

He pauses, as if realizing something. "You know he's been transferred?"

I had heard this. It's another old-timer leaving.

It's good, though. Being transferred often means moving on, possibly to treatment, and eventual release. Transfer is a moment of transition, perhaps even a milestone, for guys who don't have many such moments in their lives.

❦

After a few months of singing and interacting with volunteers in the choir, Keith was beginning to feel more human again.

Singing had always been a source of joy for him. Basic skills—reading notes, deciphering time signatures—came back to him fairly quickly. Having smoked and used drugs for years, his voice was rough, and it took time to get it back into shape. After a while, his register widened. It never became as expansive as it had been in his youth, but he was able to sing with both the second basses and the second tenors.

He made great strides as a songwriter at Oakdale. People joked about him being the resident wordsmith. Within the supportive atmosphere of the songwriting workshop, a breeze of confidence filled his sails. Knowing that people other than friends and family wanted him to succeed was heartening. Keith was used to thinking that most DOC workers didn't give 'two shlitz' about his rehabilitation. But the choir... the choir allowed you to see a better side of people.

Before this, he'd only wanted to do his time and go home. Now, he was signing on to various projects. He ran for inmate council, won, and oversaw improvements in the commissary, grooming standards, and self-betterment classes. Soon he was also on the board of New Directions, an inmate-run charity, arranging photos for inmates to send home at a reasonable price, and providing coffee for group meetings.

During rehearsals, he made it a point to help others, while trying to avoid coming across as a know-it-all. He might lean toward the person sitting next to him and gesture to them to raise their pitch to match his. One insider liked sitting by Keith because he sang loudly, while another said he didn't for the same reason. Some people would approach Keith for help, some seemed to want help but wouldn't ask, some preferred to "bull" their way through, and some only caused distractions. That was life.

The following week I catch a ride to the prison with Kevin and Maria, a couple with whom I've become friends. Maria is a special-needs teacher in a local elementary school, Kevin a campus ministry coordinator. I appreciate their politics, and I appreciate Maria's perspective on being a woman in the choir.

"I think it's important to model for these guys another way to interact with women," she says. "They don't see many females inside, so when they get out, they'll need to understand how to interact with the opposite sex in a friendly, respectful way. I guess that's one of the benefits of the choir—learning how to reconnect with all sorts of people in society."

We arrive at the prison—more geese winging their way above us—and while waiting to enter, I chat with another woman about a project she's involved in. Peg teaches English to immigrants on Wednesday evenings. She's just attended a vigil to draw attention to the arrest of a local undocumented woman and her sudden separation from her young children.

Perhaps you can tell that Oakdale choir volunteers are people who are already pretty engaged in the community. They come from a variety of backgrounds and professions. There's a professor of English. A librarian. An owner of an organic coffee business. A social worker. There's a goldsmith, whose studio shares space with a large art gallery downtown. And a professor of rhetoric, whose area of interest is animals.

A retired Mennonite minister also recently joined; I was surprised to hear he's entered the "Three-Minute Fiction Contest" on NPR's "All Things Considered" several times. He and another Mennonite, a man who works in the Parks and Rec department, drive up to Iowa City every week from Washington, Iowa, 40 minutes away.

And, because of the university's proximity, and perhaps because Mary Cohen puts the word out, there are a number of talented college students in the choir, some with amazing voices. Rose, diminutive music undergrad, is a favorite among the insiders. She sometimes steps in to direct the choir when Mary is out of town, and directed "Let There Be Peace on Earth" at our last concert. Paul enjoys teasing her about her height.

"Get up on the podium, Rose," he'll say. "Oh, you are already."

One week Keith receives permission to submit an opinion piece to the Iowa City newspaper, describing how much the choir has meant to him, how he's changed through his interactions with choir members. The column is a tribute to the idea of music as rehabilitative tool, and it generates a lot of discussion in the newspaper's online comments section. Not all of the comments are positive.

"Most of these criminals are sex offenders," one person rants, anonymously. "They're in prison to pay for their crimes, not to be singing in choirs." (Why are the most mean-spirited responses in online forums anonymous?)

"And these community members who are volunteering to sing in the choir are weak-minded and naïve; they're being taken advantage of by hardened criminals."

This attitude isn't unique, unfortunately. It reveals a swell of anger and prejudice toward those in prison, an unwillingness to forgive. There's an echo of the get-tough-on-crime stance politicians resort to in order to get elected, painting convicts as undeserving of rehabilitative efforts, to be dealt with via only the harshest of measures.

As for the claim that most choir members are sex offenders, it's likely that there are such people in the choir. Sex offenders often serve their time at Oakdale until they are transferred to another prison for treatment. There are also those who've committed other kinds of crimes. So what? All of these people are doing their time. If we accept the premise that everyone deserves a second chance, then getting hung up on the crime seems counter-productive. At least that's the ideal that many volunteers are striving to embrace; it's not always easy.

The comment also projects a bias against volunteers, suggesting that they're bleeding hearts, too quick to turn a blind eye to the reality of 'evil.'

Is this fair? Do volunteers ignore the dark places, the victims' broken-heartedness, the brutal violence in the backstory?

I don't think so. Many of the volunteers in the choir are some of the most compassionate people I've ever met. It takes strength to do this work, openness to having one's biases challenged, while holding open the possibility that people can change. I know many of them are equally concerned about the plight of crime victims. Choir members attend events during National Crime Victims' Rights Week. And our concerts often highlight the work of the Iowa Organization for Victim Assistance.

Mary Cohen reported on volunteers' experiences in a study published in 2012 by the *International Journal of Music Education*. She found significant positive attitude changes. Volunteers' experiences in the choir "shattered their stereotypes of prisoners." As one outside singer put it, "I expected them to be in shackles and not interested in singing. I quickly learned that they were human beings, had feelings, and wanted to sing." [79]

Roger, the retired Mennonite pastor, is one man with whom I've become close. His interest in prison work dates back to the 1970s, when he decided to refuse military induction. At that time, such refuseniks were often sentenced to two years at a prison farm. That didn't happen to him, but he realized that there were likely lots of people in prison who didn't have to be there and perhaps should never have been there.

"When I served as a pastor," he says, "I had many opportunities to participate in worship services in county jails and state prisons, so I learned about the prison system through these experiences. I enjoy singing, so the opportunity to sing in the Oakdale Choir seemed a good way to combine prison ministry with my interest in music. My motivation has been strengthened by the frequent appreciation expressed by the inside singers. Finally, it has been interesting to get to know the other volunteers, as I might never have met these people otherwise."

"Prisons have always seemed like a tremendous waste of money and human potential to me," he continues, "and this belief has strengthened over time. While some prisoners are undoubtedly dangerous, many others do not appear to be. If the money and effort spent on confinement could be directed toward human development and counseling, it seems to me that outcomes would be much better."

I ask him how he navigates the DOC guideline that volunteers are not there to develop friendships with the insiders.

"I've respected these guidelines and I recognize that safety and security are important concerns which can sometimes be compromised by inappropriate relationships. But any extended relationship can develop into some level of friendship and relationships with prisoners are no different. It does seem unfortunate that the DOC tries to discourage friendships as this is what most insiders seem to need, especially after they are released."

Most volunteers do seem to share a hope for the personal growth of insiders. Reflecting on the lyrics of the Swahili song *Wakati—Peace be with you my friend, til we meet again*—one outsider writes, "This is exactly what I want to say to all my inside friends. When the time comes for your new start, believe in yourself, because I have faith in you. Take pride in doing right, find in yourself the strength to persevere. And, until we meet again, whether next week or in the next life, may peace be with you, my friend."

One Tuesday evening after rehearsal, a few volunteers leave the prison and caravan to an Indian restaurant in nearby Coralville. We're hosting a visitor, Catherine Roma, who herself directs several prison choirs in Ohio. She has come to observe the OCC in action.

Conversation weaves around the table, as people respond to a question from one choir member—how can we better connect with insiders?

"Discuss the writing prompts," one person suggests.

"Ask them if they speak other languages."

"Try to find out what their jobs are."

The conversation takes a turn. One man mentions a New Yorker article he read recently entitled "How We Misunderstand Mass Incarceration."[80] It's about the increasing role prosecutors are playing in the growth of incarceration. The author, legal scholar John Pfaff, believes there are three main causes of prison growth: unregulated prosecutorial power, structural political failures, and over-long punishment of people convicted of violent crimes. But prosecutors, acting with wide discretion and little oversight, remain the engines driving mass incarceration. Appointing rather than electing prosecutors might help, this man suggests.

The food arrives—*chana masala, sag paneer*—swimming in deliciousness.

Our visitor has interesting stories to share. She tells us about a man sentenced to life in prison in one of the Ohio prisons where she volunteers. The Innocence Project—which works to free the wrongfully imprisoned—has taken up the man's case, and this touches on another aspect of prison life, the fact that some people are falsely accused, convicted and serve time—often a lot of time—for crimes they didn't commit. DNA evidence is emerging as a potent tool in overturning such convictions.

The Innocence Project doesn't take on a case unless they're convinced the accused is not guilty. Often, these convicts are poor, and people of color.

The man Cathy Roma mentions, who was wrongfully convicted, sang in one of her choirs, and wrote a song called "Black Lives Matter." The men in the choir were really into rehearsing it; the song touched them deeply.

One day, though, a deputy warden called her over and said, "You can't sing that song."

"Why not?"

"You have to sing 'All lives matter.'"

"What?!"

Exasperated, she realized she was in no position to argue. You have to be tactful in dealing with prison officials to ensure the smooth continuance of the program. So, Roma says, they sang it the way they were instructed. What else could they do? The men were dispirited by the change.

"Later, however," Roma says, "I got some friends together on the outside and we recorded the song as written. It's now on a CD."

Despite institutional inertia/racism, the song did find a place in the world. The story touched us, and as we sat around the table, we offered up hopes that, like his composition, the song's composer would soon also rediscover his place back in the world.

I thank God for the choir because you guys sparked a fire in me that I didn't know existed. Music is big down here, but I still came with an edge for songwriting and thinking outside the box. I just finished writing a song called "Change the World." There is a famous prison saying—"You don't want no smoke." When someone says this to you it means: you don't want to fight or compete. So I'm writing a song called "No Smoke" and I'm taking all the issues in the world using them as schemes of the devil, but if we pray and love each other the Devil don't want No Smoke.

— Armand

TWENTY-FOUR

On Higher Ground

JEREMY SITS IN THE rehearsal room with his feet pulled up on the rung of his chair. He yawns and stretches, a white insider with a youthful-looking face. If anyone can be said to be on the right track—he works on the choir newsletter, designs choir T-shirts, and is helping to organize the concerts—it's him.

I notice some Chinese characters glued to the front of his music folder. "What are those?"

"Those? Those are Taoist symbols. I'm really interested in Taoism."

"Really?"

"Yeah, I like the idea of being in harmony with the world around you."

Taoism is something I also have an interest in. I mention the concept of *wu wei*, action through inaction. It's about cultivating inner presence and energy, not being attached to achievement, and not getting in anyone else's face. Jeremy nods.

We talk a little more, about how traditional Taoists lived in nature and acknowledged the passing of the seasons, about the yin/yang symbol. And about how nature might not be so easily accessible in prison, but the practice of discerning the positive within the negative, and vice versa, can be pretty useful.

Passing his days with these ideas in mind seems to have inspired Jeremy. And it illuminates another, deeper, dimension of life in here.

If you define spirituality broadly—as relationship or connection to something or someone deeper or greater than your own ego-self, be that

God, or soul, or the Tao, or maybe just a commitment to values of kindness and decency—then I think you can say that most people have a spiritual life. Everyone responds to love, which is, I think, at heart what spirituality is about. Even people who appear to be in it only for themselves, who seem snared by nets of self-absorption or hatred, often turn out to be living in negative relief to spiritual ideals. That is, if you're on the run, that act of running places you in juxtaposition to what you're running from and may ultimately force a reevaluation of where you're headed.

Mary Cohen works to bring a degree of reflection into rehearsals. Recently, she's begun opening each rehearsal with a moment of quiet silence. She invites choir members to close their eyes or soften their gaze to the floor, and declare any intentions they wish for the hour and a half we're together. She sees this as a way to help members get in touch with parts of themselves they may have neglected or shut down.

The DOC allows all forms of spiritual practice in Iowa penal institutions, whether they be Buddhist, Wiccan, or Native spirituality. But Christianity, perhaps not surprisingly, is the dominant faith inside. It's often an evangelical version, emphasizing a narrative of sin and forgiveness and rebirth. I guess this, too, is not surprising, given that it speaks to the trajectory of many people's lives here—making big mistakes, and longing to be redeemed.

In a free moment near the end of one rehearsal, I find myself chatting with a man named Darnell. He tells me he used to travel around the Midwest with a bar band, every night playing a different pub, performing classic rock and country tunes.

"Sounds like fun."

He corrects me. "It was not a good life. It got me into trouble. I thank God that I'm here in prison, now." He pauses. "This is where I'm supposed to be. This is where I found the Lord. I can fulfill my destiny here."

It's stunning to hear someone say they're grateful to be inside. On the other hand, if it means an opportunity for healing, I guess I can understand it. There is a *lot* of brokenness here. Perhaps that's why AA, addiction treatment, and other 12-step programs are popular. You probably know the basic premise: *We admitted we were powerless over our addictions—that our lives had become unmanageable. We came to believe that a Power greater than ourselves could restore us to sanity. We made a decision to turn our will and our lives over to the care of God as we understood Him.*

Many insiders study the Bible, on their own or in a chaplain-led group, or through correspondence courses. And quite a few of the songs we sing in the OCC carry a Christian message— "River in Judea," for example. But most of these songs are part of a cultural canon of religious music; they're not intended to proselytize. Some of the insiders' compositions, on the other hand, are more explicitly evangelical.

Of course, with any set of religious beliefs, it sometimes happens that they may not be integrated emotionally into one's life. Religiosity—a kind of pious lip service paid to certain beliefs—manifests as distinct from spirituality, and this can have its complications. A volunteer tells me the story of a female inmate she worked with: "This woman wanted a divorce because her husband had abused their child. But her pastor told her that God didn't approve of divorce."

She continues, "I'm afraid religious volunteers may sometimes give a sense of guilt to those they're working with. They want them to feel guilty and inadequate. But doesn't God want you to love yourself, and not be a victim of psychological abuse?"

One of my correspondents, Henry, says he's found spiritual practice to be crucial in maintaining a sense of mental balance inside, as well as helping him move toward an acceptance of responsibility for what he did.

I don't know if I mentioned that I've been working with a Zen order that has a prison project. Part of the liturgy they have sent me is a Gatha of Atonement. I don't know what the average prisoner thinks he is doing here, but I think this is an opportunity to work on myself, much as I imagine monks must do.

The atonement practice he mentions is framed in Buddhist terms, and includes focusing on the following declaration: "All evil karma ever committed by me since of old on account of my beginningless greed, anger, and ignorance born of my body, mouth, and thought, I now atone for it all."

Groups like the Prison Mindfulness Institute, and Bo Lozoff's Prison Ashram Project, and the Christian-based Prison Fellowship Ministries, all offer contemplative training in prisons. Meditation, reflection, study, prayer, or *wu wei*—such practices may offer a chance to find peace, and they can be an important step in the long-term healing/growth/redemption process, shifting an insider's perspective away from the idea of simply enduring 'hard time' toward an appreciation of 'living in sacred time.'

I've been corresponding with a friend, Steven Landau, who teaches yoga and meditation in several prisons in North Carolina. Landau reminds me that yoga exercises are a good way to regulate the hormones and glands, and thus can help inmates exercise more control over their emotions, bringing more calm to their days.

He writes: *Teaching in a prison is one of the most rewarding things a yoga teacher can do. It has a distinct and positive impact on inmates' lives. And on the life of the teacher. You take someone who has little constructive activity during the day and add some spice and relaxation, and life seems worth living again.*

They don't usually practice much once they get out. They don't usually get in touch with you afterwards. But they do remember you. You notice this especially when you switch prisons you teach at, and some of the inmates remember you fondly from the last one where they were incarcerated and took some of your classes.

Things change daily without notice. Sometimes the COs call for count just before you get there and nobody shows up. But it's worth it the next time. They even learn to teach themselves and other inmates after a little while.

Most of the guys are there to stretch, relax and have a good time. Some actually have a spiritual motivation from the start.

We usually try to teach classes weekly, with yoga asanas, kiirtan and group meditation. I teach aspects of the yoga code of ethics, presented along with handouts on the Eight Limbs of Yoga. It works well to inculcate spiritual ideals into hardened or softened criminals…

One student of this type of meditation in another prison, who goes by the name of Sufi, shared in some personal correspondence his struggles to keep his mind spiritually focused, to remember that all things are sacred, as this practice teaches: "I specifically wanted to have 'thoughts of the Divine' in mind in the chow hall. But the chow hall is arguably the most chaotic atmosphere on the compound. Shoulders bump into each other in anxiety to get closer to the serving window. Prisoners continue arguments over mundane topics, discussions originating from the dorms. Guards shout for silence. Inmates cut the line to steal extra trays. Others complain to food service staff about inadequate servings."

"The motion of these always found ways to crowd my mind and leave no room for remembrance of the Divine during chewing time. Every day, as I walked out of the chow hall, I'd remember that I forgot the Divine. This continued for a while."

"One day, as I sat down to eat, I saw one of my brothers with his palms together by his chin and head bowed over his meal, and I remembered. On another occasion, I saw another brother and remembered again. Every day, just as the environment distracted me from the goal, something in it stimulated me to remember. At one point, the contact with any food in my mouth made me remember. Remembrance bounced from contact with food and the presence of it."

"The struggle to remember is helping transform my perception of my environment. The idea to see the Divine everywhere lies on my inner landscape every morning. Constant pressing of the will to remember is slowly changing my view of what was normally a distraction. The practice is powerful. Remembrance is bubbling from within me more, even without external stimuli."

One day, choir members break into small groups for a discussion on the following topic: "What does 'Always Look on the Bright Side of Life' mean to you?" I'm standing with Calvin, Amy, Lois and Chester. These small group discussions can be awkward, as sometimes people are reluctant to open up, but after a while our conversation starts to flow.

"It's like that passage in Romans," Calvin offers, "All things work together for the good for those who believe."

"I guess I can get behind that," Amy says.

Chester is thoughtful for a moment. "I look to the future," he says. "You don't really have control over what happens, but you can always look ahead for good things."

"Yes, it's like… with a positive mental outlook, you're sending good energy out into the world. You're having an impact, affecting people, and good things may come back to you." The others nod.

"They have studies which show that those people who are cheerful and joyful, they live longer," Calvin says.

"That ties in with that guy who supplemented his cancer treatment by reading lots of funny stories," says Lois. "It helped to stimulate his immune system."

"And what about laughing yoga?" Amy adds.

There's a lull in the conversation and Calvin and I drift off to one side.

"You seem to know your Bible verses."

He's quiet for a moment. "I studied for the ministry," he says. "I used to be an alcoholic, but I got cleaned up three years ago and was studying to be a minister. Then, I backslid. What happened was, my friend had vodka in the fridge inside a bottle of Mountain Dew. By mistake I drank it. After that, I figured, well, there goes three years of sobriety, I may as well keep drinking. I used it as an excuse."

Calvin's voice is full of emotion. It can't be easy for him to tell his story. The complexities of self are not easily shared, especially with a relative stranger. But amidst the high stakes of his experience, Calvin seems to have found the ability to get real. And when someone shares an intimate story of self—opening up to another person in a vulnerable, honest way—the relationship changes. The atmosphere changes, too.

"Coming to prison gave me the opportunity to get right with the Lord again. It's like, in the end it was a good thing, because I got right with God. I'm glad I came to prison."

"That *is* looking on the bright side," I say.

Like Darnell, the man who played in a bar band, Calvin sees a grander cosmic significance in his ending up inside. And who knows, maybe things do happen for a reason, and maybe lives do follow a necessary trajectory. And maybe sometimes people have to learn things the hard way.

I may not share his particular religious perspective, but as I drink in Calvin's words, I feel grateful, as if I'm sharing in something deep and true. It's almost as if a shaft of light has pierced the prison gymnasium, something out of a chiaroscuro painting, illuminating us as we stand off to the side of this group of insiders and volunteers. It's as if we're suddenly standing on higher ground.

I have been experiencing some singing in other languages myself, lately, going to Friday night services, mostly sung in Hebrew, mostly Psalms, and also attending chanting sessions, mantras in Sanskrit, twice a week. I could sing in a Catholic choir... I imagine the Catholics sing in Latin, but as I think about it, probably not. Anyway, the opportunities for delving into the religious traditions are endless. I guess that says something else about prison. A writer I just learned about, Ilona Karmel, said, "Man lives in constant tension between contradictory forces within himself, above all what I would call 'the everyday and the Sabbath,' his awareness of himself as he is, and his longing for what he wants to become."

— Henry

TWENTY-FIVE

What Makes You Happy?

A S WE ENTER THE prison today, a few artistically inclined inmates are gathered in one of the main corridors, painting murals on the walls. "Honor Those Who Serve," reads a newly stenciled banner stretching across the top of one wall. From the opposite side an eagle screeches down upon us, its talons extended fiercely. Mottoes of the various military branches curl beneath some of the paintings. Pencil markings suggest the ghostly outline of soldiers, while more fully realized Marines gaze nobly down on us as we walk past.

Support for the military runs strong here. Some of the COs are former military. A POW-MIA flag, with the words "They are not forgotten" flies below the American flag in front of the prison. And a lot of insiders have served, or come from families with members who have.

In fact, one of our inside singers has written a song about his father receiving the silver star for bravery during WW II. Its lyrics echo in my mind as we march toward the rehearsal room.

My father was a good man, for this I do know, A lad of only twenty, in the army he did go. To fight for his country in a land far away from home, He found himself in Germany, so young and all alone...

Then one fateful day, they went out on patrol, suddenly bullets were flying, the men lost all control.

Courageously defying fate, determined to survive, my father led them through the night, he brought them back alive...

The men move aside as we pass, gripping their brushes, one artist's face beaming with pride.

It's cool in the rehearsal room. Terence says it'll be cold one day, and hot the next, and that it varies from place to place within the prison. He jokes that whoever's in charge of heating just spins a giant wheel to see who gets what.

I take a seat near Dylan, who wants to teach me Italian. In the last year he's tackled a little bit of French, Spanish, and Italian, not to mention Chinese, through books from the prison library.

"*Prego. Multo bene. Como stai?* Italian's a lot like Spanish," he says. "I'm learning how to order food."

The chatter dies down as Mary steps onto her podium and calls for our attention.

"I want to share something I learned recently," she says. "I happened to listen to a Ted Talk, and the speaker said that if you're feeling nervous, or unsure, you can do a bold movement, something like this." She shoots an arm into the air above her head, her other arm clinched next to her abdomen, kung fu style.

"Heeyah!"

We practice it, laughing. Mary says she was inspired to do these "power poses" (most of which are more serious than the kung fu pose) by social psychologist Amy Cuddy, who speaks about how expansive, open postures can affect feelings and behaviors. When people feel more powerful, Cuddy asserts, they have the ability to see challenges as opportunities.

I think this is one reason why the posture we assume when we sing - spine straight, shoulders back, head raised - is so good for us. This is just one of the warm-ups Mary offers, aimed at giving us more confidence and ease in our singing. She follows the lead of her grad school professor, Dr. James Daugherty, in developing an appropriate warm-up sequence: a focus on alignment, breathing, physical warm-up, and vocalizing, starting with high pitches and moving to descending phrases.

She also incorporates ideas from the Alexander Technique: allow your head to delicately balance on your spine, let your back lengthen and widen, allow your neck to rest free. This sequence ties in to the idea of embodiment-as-enrichment at the heart of her research.

We continue with more warm-ups, stretching tight muscles, loosening arms and legs, cracking stiff necks. We are a stiff-necked people.

"Run your fingers down both sides of your face," Mary instructs. "Feel its tallness—this will bring depth to the notes you sing."

"Also, express joy in your face," she encourages.

Paul pipes up, "That's why I grew a beard!"

With an eye on finalizing the program for the spring concert, we rehearse "Man in the Mirror," a song popularized by Michael Jackson. The lyrics suggest that if you want to make the world a better place, you start by working on yourself. A guy named Dan is standing next to me; he leans over and sing-whispers, "I'm starting with the Dan in the Mirror."

I choke back a laugh. "Nice sentiment," I tell him, "but please don't sing it that way in the concert."

"Why not?"

"'Cuz you'll crack me up."

He smiles.

Many of us of a certain age and taste in comedy recognize the next song, "Always Look on the Bright Side of Life," by Eric Idle. It's a song Mary wrestled over including, since in its original incarnation it was sung in a Monty Python movie while Idle was cheerfully being crucified on a cross.

"It might offend some people," Mary says. "But they did do it at the Olympics. And it is hilarious."

None of us seem to have a problem with it. There's an extra layer of irony in doing the song here, but the positive message is undeniable. And it's so silly that it feels really good to sing.

If life seems jolly rotten, there's something you've forgotten, and that's to laugh and smile and dance and sing. When you're feeling in the dumps, dooon't be silly, chumps, just purse your lips and whistle, that's the thing!

The dogs sprawling under the chairs perk up; they love this. A few people link arms and perform leg kicks at the big finale, and Dylan does a little *Monty Python and the Holy Grail* horse dance, clapping his hands together as if he were holding half coconuts and prancing in place. Some days there's just something in the air.

We take a crack at Chester's tango piece, which he premiered during the songwriting workshop concert. The song's rhythm invokes images of gypsy women in black ruffled dresses with rose stems clenched in their teeth. In a moment of spontaneity, Karletta steps forward and stomps her foot like a flamenco dancer. In response, Mary approaches her, and the two of them extend their arms, clasp hands and dance cheek to cheek across the room in long strides, giddy with laughter.

Time to settle down. From the ridiculous we move to the sublime: Roland rolls his wheelchair up to the piano, and begins a duet with Karletta. He plays with such fervor, such soul, that the mood in the room changes. He and Karletta trade off singing verses, and suddenly the room is as charged as an old-time revival tent. His bright soulful chords pull movement from our feet.

We then move on to practice "Happiness" from the musical *Scrooge*, which contains the line *"Happiness is whatever you want it to be."* The solo on this is sung by Jude, a white insider in his thirties, who's new to the choir. As he lifts his head and flexes his jaw, a rich warm baritone sound pours out of his mouth. Fellow tenor Tanner and I turn to each other, eyebrows raised. The guy can sing.

Toward the end of rehearsal we enter the circle, the unbroken circle, and, at the prompting of Mary's question—*What makes you happy?*—we each offer a response. There are some repetitions, some sentimental favorites. And while the physical parameters shaping the exercise are altered for about half of us, the responses are revealing in their universality.

"Friends."

"Family."

"The Lord."

"Not much," Shannon says, and people groan.

"Obama!" someone shouts, and the man next to me rolls his eyes.

"Love of God."

"Food!" Armand calls out.

"The Tigers beating the Yankees."

"Eating Armand's food!"

"Music."

"Making music."

"Singing in community."

One man breaks into a brief, slightly discomfiting, soliloquy: "Knowing that life is temporary and I'm going to be in heaven with my father someday and have eternal life." But then someone calls out, "Speech!" and people laugh.

The circle spills into a number of dyads and triads, and we mill around for a few moments, chatting, before being herded out the door.

Have a good evening, everyone! Drive safely! As we shuffle out, Paul adds: "Drive fast! The state needs the revenue!"

On the long walk down the hall, I turn to one of the activity coordinators, "How's your kid?"

"She's good, she's nine months old now. And has an obstinate streak."

"Takes after her parents?"

"Yeah, after both of us."

Passing through the security doors, I catch up with Kevin. He's musing over our last song. "In my opinion, the lyrics to 'Happiness' don't really reflect what happiness is. Happiness is not whatever you want it to be. Happiness is right relationship with something deep." OK, fair enough.

In the foyer, we all bundle up, pulling on jackets, retrieving keys and wallets and purses from the lockers.

And we're out of the building and into the night. A blanket of fog envelops the prison. With the security lights sweeping the gloom, the scene could be a futuristic film set. Or, perhaps, the airport scene at the end of 'Casablanca.'

This could be the beginning of a beautiful friendship.

"Watching Over Me" is a song I wrote about my great grandmother. Every song I've written is personal, but this one is closer to me. Writing the song was easy, but emotionally it was difficult. Gram was the Matriarch of the family. Remembering her fills me with sadness but with immense joy at the same time. A lot of people connect the song with their own lives. It's a beautiful feeling.

— Keith

TWENTY-SIX

Crossing the Line

THESE DAYS I'M TRYING to carpool to choir as much as possible. Lois is busy with work today and unable to attend, so I meet fellow choir member Tricia at her house and we drive to pick up her husband Pete at his place of work. Pete folds his six-foot-four frame into their minivan and munches on an apple Tricia has brought him while she maneuvers down I 80 and we talk about what we've been up to. Like many choir members, they're busy people. Pete is on the "Friends of Hickory Hill Park" board; Tricia is helping to start the "Artifactory" Center for the Arts.

The big news, though, is that Everett's in solitary.

"He has a real anger problem, I guess," Tricia tells me. "Apparently, he blows up about once a day. But he had been getting better at managing his anger, so this is a tough break."

In this instance, someone jostled Everett while he was in the hallway trying to talk to his brother on the phone, and he lost his cool.

"Some cleaning guy was making too much noise," Tricia says, "and he couldn't hear his brother. He got mad at the guy, and carried it around until the next day, when he got into a confrontation with him. He ended up with a broken nose himself, and got sent to the hole. Now he might be transferred out."

Solitary is used with discretion at Oakdale, Warden McKinney has told me, and not for long periods. All prisons need it, he claims, for certain individuals, including those who might engage in self-harm. Long-term solitary confinement has been criticized by groups such as the American Friends Service Committee as a violation of human rights. It can have debilitating physical and psychological effects.[81]

At Oakdale, McKinney says, those placed in solitary stay there until they can be safely handled again, usually no more than ten or fifteen days. The situation saddens me. Everett's a good guy. Now he might miss this season's concerts, and he might even be gone for good.

But during the next rehearsal several guys tell me that Everett's already out of solitary, and has gone before the classification board, and he might be able to join us for the concert.

The following Tuesday, Everett shows up, and sits at the end of the row. I catch his eye and wave. He waves back. Good, I think, he'll be joining us in time for the performance. But I have to concentrate on the music, and after a while when I look over again, I don't see him anywhere.

It turns out he had only come to return his sheet music—he's being transferred to another prison. This is not necessarily a good thing. He's being sent to some place with a higher security rating to serve out the rest of his sentence, a place without many of the privileges he enjoyed at Oakdale. And it will probably be a place without something like the choir.

He'd come to rehearsal because he'd wanted to say goodbye to his fellow singers. Mary was going to take a moment to acknowledge him, but got distracted with rehearsal matters.

And then he was gone.

On our next week's drive to the prison, Tricia, Pete and I discuss Everett's anger issues, and other choir developments. "Anthony hasn't shown up for a while. He has such a great voice. I wonder what happened." There are many reasons an insider might stop attending, including health concerns, conflicts with other prisoners, being transferred (like Everett), or other activities scheduled at the same time.

"I heard he wants to become an opera singer, and he's saving his voice."

"That doesn't make sense—wouldn't he want to exercise his voice, to practice?"

"Yeah, well…"

In addition to participating in the choir, Tricia and Pete spend some weekends at the prison with the Alternatives to Violence Project (AVP), a program that brings trained volunteers in to work with insiders on developing ways to deal with their anger and manage their feelings. Everett had been a participant.

AVP is "an experiential program, helping people learn skills and attitudes that can lead to lives free of violence. The basic workshop introduces conflict resolution skills. Step by step exercises focus on Affirmation, Communication, Cooperation and Creative Conflict Resolution," according to the AVP brochure. Advanced workshops take a deeper plunge into the issues of Stereotyping, Power, Fear, Anger, Gender Issues and Forgiveness.

"We do things like trust exercises," Tricia tells me as she exits onto the highway leading to Oakdale. "One very large man really liked one of the exercises—falling backward off a table into the arms of his compatriots!"

"Of course, during these exercises, a lot of stuff comes up. The insiders have built this wall around their emotions, they're holding everything in. Lots of them had trauma growing up—parents who didn't care for them, or who were doing drugs. So they've shoved everything down. When we do the exercises, all this stuff starts to come up and sometimes, it's hard for them to manage."

To counter this heaviness and help the men feel more at home in their bodies, they do a series of exercises known as "Light and Lively." This incorporates a lot of the games people played as kids. For example, you form a bridge with two sets of arms and a guy has to pass underneath them. They love this silly stuff, Tricia says, and there's always a lot of laughter.

Keith has confirmed for me the value of AVP. "It sounded like a good thing, and honestly I thought it would look good to the parole board. Some of the concepts I had experience with when I was younger and was a conflict manager in middle school, and a peer helper in high school. It's really about trying to create an environment and society where everyone is treated fairly."

"I really enjoyed my first workshop," he continues, "and I've taken and facilitated numerous workshops since. I can't understand why it's not in every prison. It's all handled by volunteers. Concepts are learned through role playing, sharing of personal experience and any form outside the box. It's free and it works. So, of course the state administrators don't like it."

AVP does seem like a powerful program for learning to deal with anger, and for learning to shift how you perceive others. A friend, Clare Novak, shared with me her experience volunteering with AVP in another prison.

I was standing in the guardhouse outside Lovelock Correctional Center: eager to go in, but anxious. I'd been waiting for months to take part in the

Alternatives to Violence Project—its Basic workshops are held only in prisons. So I crossed through the steel gates and barbed wire fences into a territory that was unreal to me except through my required training from the Department of Corrections and years of shadowy, scary movies.

And over the next three days, that unreality, that fear, those shadows, were replaced by something surprising and profound.

It started when we had to introduce ourselves: the 20 male inmates who had waited months (some, years) to participate in the workshop; the nine inmates trained as facilitators; the two female volunteers; and me: the oldest participant; the only one from the "outside."

"Give yourself a nickname by choosing an adjective that starts with the same letter as your first name," Nifty Nancy said. I looked around the circle. I have to keep my guard up; I've been trained not to trust these guys. Compassionate Clare might sound too vulnerable, I thought. So I went with Curious Clare.

But then I heard the inmates choose their names: Kind Kent. Mellow Michael. Jovial Jon. Even Poetic Pete. What will I hear around this circle, I began to wonder? Who do I assume is here—and who is really here?

The breakthrough revelation for me came when we shared an exercise called "Crossing the Line." Magnificent Marc rolled a rope across the center of the room and asked us all to gather against the far wall.

"When I read a statement," he said, "cross the line to the opposite side of the room if it is true for you. Face the others who did not cross. Look around and ask yourself, are there any surprises?"

Cross the line if you: Were in the military. Went to college. Have traveled outside the U.S. Grew up in a stable family. Were in a family with drug or alcohol problems. Were ever told not to cry. Ever had someone give up on you.

Each time I crossed the line at these statements and more, I was surprised by who was around and across from me. And I acknowledged each slight shock as a sign of my ignorant assumptions based on the men's looks, age, race, tattoos, accents—how I thought society worked.

Why did I assume that the biggest guys would be the toughest guys? That all inmates would have a similar negative history: badly educated or touched by addiction or by domestic violence?

Why did I assume I would be somehow superior or set apart? That these men and I would not share common hurts and strengths?

And each time I crossed the room, I began to regret the line that separated me from the men with whom I had just shared common ground. As we silently grouped and regrouped, making revelations to each other by where we stood, we paused and looked deeply into each other's faces.

We connected.
We became real to each other.

Patrick, too, has been transferred.

He writes from his new prison that the transfer has been a great hardship. *I left behind three groups of people that were very important to my life for over two years. One was the writers workshop, one was the songwriters workshop, and, of course, the choir itself. There is nothing here to replace any of them. The living conditions are worse, the opportunities fewer, friendships less numerous, the rules more petty, the officers less human, and my life in general less tolerable. Even my health has suffered.*

Pain and swelling in his right leg was diagnosed as cellulitis and treated with antibiotics by the prison doctor.

He went back to work for six days before the swelling increased dramatically, the pain returned, and some bruising followed. Sent to the hospital in Iowa City, it took them just three minutes to diagnose a deep vein thrombosis—an acute blood clot—just below his knee. He had walked on this leg for almost four weeks due to the misdiagnosis of the previous doctor.

Now he is out of work for at least another thirty days. No work means no money, and no vitamins or any way to supplement the diet provided by the institution. This diet, he writes, is "based almost completely on calories with no regard for human needs for protein, vitamins, minerals, etc." It doesn't bode well for the future.

Ruminating on the quality of food and medical diet inside, Patrick continues,

Cream of sweat sock soup is what we call the liquid diet here.

I agree that healthier diet would probably mean better health for the inmates, but that will never happen. First off, they will tell you that we get a healthy diet, 3,000 calories per day. Unfortunately, much of that comes from starch and carbs. We get three pieces of fresh fruit per week and some canned fruit, but the canned stuff is bottom of the barrel variety, a grade below generic store brands. In fact, much of the food we get is donated or sold at low cost because it cannot be distributed to the general public. The boxes the pizza comes in are marked "Not to be served in public schools." They can't serve it to kids, but they can sure serve it to us!

Another reason is the ever-popular budget crisis. When the DOC's budget is cut, one of the first things to be reduced is the food budget. This is a large

expense, one of the biggest costs of housing inmates. It is also an area where costs can be "trimmed" without affecting anything but the inmates' stomachs. If inmates complain? Oh well. Inmates complain about everything anyway. (Sadly, there is some truth to this.)

The menu is supposed to be standardized across the state. What we eat tomorrow should be the same as what the inmates in Rockwell City are eating. This is partially true. The problem is that not all the food is purchased at the state level. Much of it is purchased at institution discretion. The chicken served here may differ greatly in size and quality from what is served in Clarinda. The same goes for vegetables. The broccoli we get is 99 percent stalks. Rarely have I seen a floret among the stems.

The recipes also differ from institution to institution. The tater tot casserole was good in Newton, but terrible here. The kitchen staff have a lot to do with it as well. Some are more concerned with quality than others. Most of the vegetables we get are cooked until all the nutritional value has been boiled out.

This is not to say that all meals here are bad. Perhaps two days a week we will get a meal that tastes good and is filling. But 2/21 isn't really a good average. More often, we are forced to eat things that are not appealing or be hungry. Sometimes both! Enough complaining. (For now.)

TWENTY-SEVEN

Courage

ONE DAY HALFWAY THROUGH the season I get some bad news. An old friend of mine, feeling sick and lonely and desperate, has taken her own life.

The shock, the incomprehensibility of this, roils through my body and leaves me gasping. I ask myself what I could have done to help her. She was bright, an artist and poet, but she also struggled with mental illness, substance abuse, and poverty, exactly the kinds of things I've been coming into contact with in the prison. Her death is a stark reminder of the daily pain so many people seem to live with.

As I sit with my grief, the days slowly wending by, the lyrics to one of this friend's favorite songs—by Lucinda Williams—echo in my brain: "See what you missed when you left this sweet old world." If anything had made her life worth living for a time, it was music. And if anything allows me to shift the pain of the loss a little, perhaps it is singing with my choir friends.

Sadly, other losses are occurring in our tribe around the same time. A tragic car accident takes the life of the daughter of stalwart choir couple, Steve and Lora, and choir members move to enfold them in support of their grief, offering hugs and a listening presence.

A prisoner I've been corresponding with, Henry, whose lyrical reflections punctuate the chapters of this book, has become ill. His kidneys are failing. Before the season is out, he, too, will pass. As much pain as he's in, perhaps it's for the best, but it's difficult news to receive.

Dying in prison strikes me as a particularly sad transition. Though no insider choir members have passed this year, some General Population prisoners have. And when a person dies at Oakdale, the insider hospice volunteers are permitted to wear bright tie-dye T-shirts for three days. When you see insiders walking the halls in these T-shirts, it's a sobering signal. The gesture signifies recognition of a life, a shift from the drabness of daily routine to a more vivid acknowledgement of one of the experiences the inside has in common with the outside: time shuffles forward, we lose our physical vitality, and we all pass into whatever lies beyond this world.

And then, today. The room falls quiet as Mary Cohen stands before us. It's taken some time before she was able to share this story, but now she explains how her older sister was driving early one morning last year in Washington, D. C., when a car crossed the median, the driver having fallen asleep at the wheel, and hit her straight on, killing her instantly. Her two prize show dogs were in the car with her, and one of them was also killed.

"She loved those dogs," Mary says, quietly. "They were German short-hair pointers, Brunhilde and Siegfried. She used to put a tiara on Brunhilde and dance around with her."

We can hear something, a catch, in Mary's voice. Her role has always been to model positivity for us, but sometimes positivity is elbowed out of the way by something else.

"My sister always inspired me," she continues. "I did whatever she did. Her motto was 'find the joy.' I tried to do this, too, but I struggled to find the joy after such a horrible tragedy."

In the midst of her grief, Mary says, she focused on her sister's approach to life. She remembered the wonderful things about her. And, like the insiders in the songwriters' workshop who express their pain through lyric, she wrote a song. It took muddling through the grieving process for a while before she could craft the lyrics.

> *How can I find the joy when brick walls block my path?*
> *How can I find the joy when I'm living through the aftermath?*
> *Joy is rooted in compassion, compassion comes from love.*
> *But tell me, what are the seeds of love?*

The song speaks to me as well, as I take steps to honor the memory of my friend. The choir will perform it at our next concert, singing an intimate song of grief back to the person whose story it represents, surrounding our director, who has given so much to the choir, with the healing power of song.

Weeks pass. The cold weather begins to dissipate; some afternoons the sky is streaked with purple and the sun warms us as we enter the prison. Today, while walking through the metal detector, I remember at the last moment that I have keys in my pocket, so I fish them out, step out of line and run to put them in a locker. Back in line, we walk the halls softly, single file, and when we reach the rehearsal room, the sectionals are already underway.

Mary divides the choir into two groups, and each sings a chromatic scale, one heading up the scale and one climbing slowly down. Our voices pass each other in the middle, and the intervals are gorgeous. As if that weren't challenging enough, we divide into four groups and repeat the exercise, starting every two notes. It's striking, and difficult, and beautiful. I don't think we would have been able to do this a few years ago.

Karl and Armand have been busy between rehearsals, polishing one of Armand's new songs. Leaving their seats, they make their way to the front of the room to introduce it to us. The insiders keep up with the news, of course, and this song addresses a horrific recent school shooting in which young children were killed. Karl opens with soulful guitar riffs, followed by Armand's hip-hop incantation.

Can someone explain all these tragedies?
What good are our eyes if it's all that they see?
What words can you say to relieve what I've lost?
When there's no gift to give which will cover the cost
There's no medicine that will ease my heartache.

Some of us have moist eyes as we applaud. And Armand surprises us by launching into an impromptu speech. "You know, you outsiders, you could do more to combat gun violence," he says. "You could do things like go to schools and talk with the kids."

The moment is poignant. We've experienced several moments of deep feeling this season, and this song, like Mary's, seems to express something many of us are struggling with. Tyrone raises his hand and says, "You know, there's a certain attitude in here, that you don't show your feelings. But I can't say that I won't be breaking down in tears after singing that song."

A little later in the rehearsal, Jeremy gets up and goes to stand next to the portable CD player. Mary gives him a nod. He inserts a disc, presses *play*, and after a moment a female voice—warm and resonant—radiates from the speakers. The voice climbs gently up the scale:

I wish you courage for the next step and the step, I wish you peace in the middle of the storm. I wish you unexpected joy, the strength to see you through, and a heart wide open to all the love surrounding you.

This is Barbara McAfee, a vocal musician who leads a hospice choir in Minneapolis. Later I'll take a workshop on singing for hospice patients with this woman, and be struck by her presence and her playfulness, as she emphasizes that hospice, like prison, is a setting where a little bit of compassion goes a long way.

Right now, though, Mary has something up her sleeve. She invites us to take part in an exercise: "Begin moving to the rhythm of this song, walk around the room, and engage with each person in your path. Offer a greeting, a smile, a handshake, or maybe a silent wish for each other's welfare."

The point is to acknowledge, gracefully and gratefully, everyone we encounter. And, in the spirit of the song, wish them courage and peace for the next step, and the next.

"I don't get it," says Ronald, who's standing next to me. "What are we supposed to do?"

"Umm, just go around and smile at everybody."

But I understand Ronald's uncertainty; it's not such an easy thing we're being asked to do, to open our hearts, especially here.

The music starts up again. Everyone begins to move, taking steps to the beat of the song, swaying back and forth a little, nodding and smiling at each other as we pass. What seems easiest is to bump fists with each person, which adds a little structure to the exercise, while looking into the eyes of those who are open to it. I pass Lora, who seems to be radiating kindness. There's Steve, smiling, and Jeremy with a shy grin. Some of the men look a bit uncomfortable.

On one level, of course, all we're doing is walking around the room, tracing meandering paths across a big circle. And it's possible to do that without risking anything. But I think in a small way within this exercise, and perhaps in a larger way over the course of our time in the choir, what we're really doing is making ourselves vulnerable, and with that vulnerability can come opening.

Eventually the song comes to an end, and everyone is standing in a new place. We go around the circle and speak our names.

The exercise is both awkward and powerful, and it gets me thinking. What next steps have I taken as a result of being part of the Oakdale Choir?

How have I changed, how have I stepped up to integrate the energies we've generated here?

Well, I've certainly learned a lot about prison issues and restorative justice, which I've tried to express and share in this book.

But on a more personal level, the exercise has me feeling into something I've been grappling with these past few years, and that is how important it is to walk through a room—to walk through the world, really—shouldering a sense of compassion, not a mind bent on analyzing every interaction. This has often been my challenge, to step outside my head, into my body, and connect.

I've had opportunities to practice this, since every week we enter this room and make an effort to relate to each other. I'd like to think I've become more accepting of people as they are, where they are, without judgment.

I like what Martin Buber, the Jewish philosopher, has to say in this regard: we have an opportunity to interact with everyone we meet as either an "it" or a "Thou." [82]The former, of course, objectifies the other person, reduces them; the latter sees the sacred within a person. Creating an "I-Thou" relationship thus deepens and enriches every aspect of life.

So I've worked at becoming more fully present to the people in my immediate orbit, my tenor-sphere, right around me. One insider, whose political leanings have revealed themselves over time to be pretty much diametrically opposed to mine, has nevertheless become someone with whom I genuinely enjoy spending time, just hanging out and joking together between songs. It's an interaction that might not have happened on the outside. We've come to recognize something deeper in each other, an in-the-moment spark of soul.

The beauty of this group, I'm coming to understand, is that it allows all of us—whatever our level of self-understanding, whatever issues we're struggling with—to listen to each other. Listening is an under-rated art. When we offer our attention to someone else, dropping any preconceived notions we might have, our sense of having to be right, or having to prove anything, drops away.

Life is fleeting and fragile. Our friends and loved ones will one day be gone. We're all struggling to find our way. But it braces me to see how, exercising our vulnerability and courage in this way, walking through our little corner of the world, we can't help but learn from each other.

Thich Nhat Hanh writes of a morning walk he took in early spring in the south of France, where he notices the flowers along the path and thinks how beautiful they will look on the altar during the next service he leads. That evening a late storm removes them from the landscape. But only for a week or so. Once again he is walking along the same path. He interrogates the flowers he sees—'Are you the same flowers I saw before, or are you new and different?'

What is it that gives substance to the becoming, deepens the depth, enriches the memories of unfolding life? If not loveliness, then what? The knowledge of transience, I think.

Spirit? Soul? Loveliness? Beauty? Whatever these things mean, I would like to have a little more of them in my life. A little more wisdom would be nice as well.

— Henry

TWENTY-EIGHT

The Problem of Neighbors

D URING HIS FIRST STRETCH inside, Patrick found religion. He learned about and applied to participate in a program at a prison in Newton, Iowa, called InnerChange Freedom Initiative (a program which has since been discontinued).

For twenty months he lived on E Unit, a 200-man honor dorm where prisoners had keys to their cells and daily access to the yard and other privileges. They agreed to give up TV, cussing, and some free time in order to remain in the program. Patrick immersed himself in study, prayer, and coursework. He began singing and started a Christian rock band, writing lyrics to dozens of songs. My sense is that he experienced a real turn-around and wanted to start life afresh.

Upon his release, volunteers provided him with an apartment, furniture, clothing, food, a phone, a job, and a church to attend. He began preaching part-time, and traveled to Missouri to lecture at a Christian college, drawing on his experiences to illustrate his sermons.

But by 2005, things had begun to unravel in his life. Two of his closest friends died. He lost his apartment and had to move in with someone and pay more in rent. His band broke up. Then, during one week in December of 2007, things took a sharp turn for the worse. Two weeks before Christmas, three more friends died over the course of five days. Patrick was devastated.

During the week of the memorial services and the weeks to come, he turned to drugs again, trying to outrun his grief. On February 15, 2008, at about 9:30 at night, a detective came to his house and charged him with 2nd degree sexual abuse for allegedly touching the genital area of a housemate's five-year old daughter. This allegation was made by the child's mother, who said she witnessed it with her own eyes.

He sat in county jail, awaiting trial, trying to figure out what had happened. (He continues to maintain his innocence on this charge.) The woman owed him a large amount of money. She had lost her job, and blamed him. Patrick also claims that she knew her daughter was being molested by a family member, and she was unwilling to prosecute that person.

In Iowa, as in most states since the '90s, an accusation of child abuse is basically the same as a conviction. No evidence is necessary. And there was no evidence in this case, just the mother's statement and the daughter's agreement with that statement.

No doubt, Patrick had been moving with the wrong crowd again, sinking into old habits, and it was only a matter of time before something caught up with him. But he was surprised at this turn of events.

I'd had friendly conversations with the guy who came around on his monthly mission to spray the kitchen and bathroom floors of my apartment for pests, a practice mandated by the landlord. I never noticed anything strange about him. We chatted about the weather, mostly. One day, though, a new person came to spray.

"Where's the guy who usually comes?" I asked.

"Him? He's in a load of trouble."

He told me the man had exposed himself near a school, and was now in jail.

What the...? How did a person come to do such a thing?

Sexual crime is, to put it mildly, a highly charged issue. Trust plays such an important role in the realm of sexuality, and when that trust is violated—when a person's vulnerability is exploited—a sacred line gets crossed. And when children are taken advantage of, some would say the action borders on being unforgivable.

But it's also true that most sex offenders are damaged people, with heavy emotional impairments, and that they suffer from addictions. And like all addicts—although they need to take responsibility for their actions—they need treatment.

The issue certainly makes people uncomfortable. I remember following a conversation on a Facebook page set up for members of a small Midwestern town where friends of mine lived. A registered sex offender, a former abuser of children, was moving to the town, and people were freaking out. The comment thread included threats of physical violence against the man, and angry diatribes about the fact that he would be living in the community. Only one person noted that the man had served his time and gone through treatment, and this perspective was widely criticized.

I've got questions. Can sex offenders be reformed? Should they all be lumped into one category? Do we define people by the single worst thing they've done? Does putting people away in harsh conditions, and then stigmatizing them after their release, solve the problem? Or does it create new problems?

For answers, I turned to several sources, including Karla Miller. In an earlier chapter I mentioned a conversation I had with Miller about how prisoners can be manipulative. She has a lot to say about the issue of sex offenders, as well. Miller was director of the Rape Victim Advocacy Program in Iowa City for 22 years. She's now a trauma therapist and consultant, and works with sex offenders, including some at Oakdale.

People think sex offenders make up a homogenous group, but there are distinct differences according to types, motivations, and whom they pick as victims, Miller says. By the time they're in their twenties, many offenders have a long history of deviant behavior. They've developed justifications for, and patterns of denial of, their behavior. They share certain characteristics—being secretive, hiding their deviancy, minimizing, and selfishness. They're self-centered in terms of what they perceive their needs to be. And it's hard for them to change.

Offenders may come from a family with a history of trans-generational sex abuse, where abnormality becomes normal. They can use this as an excuse. But as Miller points out, lots of people were abused who didn't grow up to commit sex crimes. Taking personal responsibility, and making the right choices, is crucial.

Whether or not someone acts on their impulse may depend on how they're feeling about themselves, their ability to control their own lives, and how other people perceive them. Some feel a compulsion. They've chosen sex as a way to act out, and they start planning their attack.

Miller also leads training for volunteers, teaching them how not to be manipulated, and helping them understand why people act out. When a released offender of children receives support from a church community, for example, there has to be accountability, an earning of trust. Things need to be spelled out; at a church dinner, the man shouldn't be hanging out with the kids.

Education is important. Some people are able to change, once they understand the impact of what they've done. Development of empathy for the victim can help them manage their behavior. Some offenders care about how people see them, and respond to social pressure and status. For others, who don't care about their impact, things can be trickier.

Sex offender treatment is still a relatively young field, around only since 1984. According to Miller, treatment focuses on developing understanding of key topics: life skills, relationships, communication, sexuality and appropriate behavior. Offenders often have a history of anxiety, compulsion, or depression. Medication can be useful, but it can also have side effects; one med lowers testosterone with the side effects of weight gain or breast development.

Supervision is critical, adds Daniel Craig, the Deputy Director of IDOC. "Ongoing oversight and programming doesn't stop. We evaluate the risk for them going back into the community. There are varying levels of risk, and we keep tabs on the riskiest. It's hard for the public to accept them once they return to the community. A lot of what these people did was done in secret, so it's hard for the trust to come back."

Once released, people are expected to attend weekly meetings for two to three years. Group work is the best mode of treatment, Miller says, because especially for males, "They can call each other on their BS. There's usually a male and a female facilitator. These guys have generally had bad relationships with women. This way they learn that women are human, and can learn to behave differently with them."

Miller rues the fact that treatment programs are being cut. With fewer treatment options, people tend to lapse into dysfunctional behavior and disease, and it costs more to treat in the long run.

Unfortunately, she says, there's grim prognosis for a cure for some kinds of sex offenders. A few age out. Some receive enough support in the community that they're able to restrain themselves. Engaging in pro-social activities, like art and music, is very important. It may not always be enough to stop offenders in the first place, but it can show them that they can develop their lives in a different direction.

"Fill their lives with pro-social stuff and it reduces the risk," Miller says.

"They can learn to meet their psychological needs in a different way."

Patrick was convicted and sentenced on the sexual abuse charge, and came to Oakdale, after which, as we've seen, he joined the choir, and was later transferred out for treatment. I've learned he's someone who tries to understand things deeply, especially when they affect him personally. He's done a lot of research on the issue of sexual offenses and, in our correspondence, he details the seemingly excessive restrictions sex offenders face once they're released, restrictions that make it very difficult for them to work, find housing, or have any kind of life at all.

"Once I've discharged my sentence," he writes, "my 'special sentence' begins. I will have 'done my time,' but will still be on parole for the *rest of my life. Any* offense will send me back to prison for a minimum of two years. (This includes traffic offenses.) In addition, I cannot drink any alcohol or enter a tavern for the rest of my life. The criminal justice system has taken the group of offenders *least* likely to reoffend (other than murderers), and saddled them with impossible limitations, guaranteeing repeat customers. Ninety-nine percent of sex offenders who come back to prison come for a parole violation, not a new crime."

Some states have decided that harsher laws are not always better. Iowa, for example, no longer has the 2000-foot law (which keeps sex offenders from living near schools). The vast majority of sex offenders take their victims from among acquaintances or family; abduction of school kids, while sensational and covered heavily by media, is rare. The law now focuses on restricting certain areas such as swimming pools or schools. Iowa has also sharply reduced the number of sex offenses for which residency restrictions—prohibitions against living in certain areas—apply.

"Ask any law enforcement officer what the 2000-foot law does," Patrick says, "and he's likely to tell you, 'Nothing.' The truth is, it *does* do something. It severely limits the ability of sex offenders to find a place to live, and increases the likelihood that they will fail. No home? No job? No phone? No money to pay fines? No transportation to treatment or parole appointments? All of these lead the same place—right back to prison. And the cycle starts over again."

Every state keeps a register, and many people assume that anyone on a sex offender registry is a rapist or child molester. But Sarah Tofte of Human Rights Watch found that at least five states require men to register if they were caught visiting prostitutes. [83] At least thirteen states required it for urinating in public. Twenty-nine states required registration for teenagers who had consensual sex with another teenager. And thirty-two states registered flashers and streakers. This helps to explain why the number of registered sex offenders in America has exploded.

"There's a philosophy that sex offenders are all the same," Rachel Marie-Crane Williams opines. "There's no nuance in the way we treat sex offenders. It's terrible. The registry does not keep anyone safer. Sex offenders have done their time, so why continue to punish them?"

Karla Miller, on the other hand, thinks the registry is an excellent idea. She believes that without it, offenders will simply go to another state that doesn't have registries or background checks. She believes we should let the community know that a sex offender is in the area. Secrecy is their greatest friend, she says. The one problem she does acknowledge is that a person who is mistakenly placed on the registry will find it very difficult to be removed.

But some studies do suggest that making it harder for sex offenders to find a home or a job makes them likelier to reoffend. Kristen Zgoba of the New Jersey Department of Corrections found that the state's system for registering sex offenders and warning their neighbors cost millions of dollars and had no discernible effect on the number of sex crimes.[84]

In line with these findings, Human Rights Watch urges a scaling back of registries. Those convicted of minor offenses should not be required to register, says Tofte. Nor should juveniles. Sex offenders need to be individually assessed, and only those judged likely to rape or abuse a child should be registered. She believes the information on sex-offender registries should be held by the police, and not published online.

The challenge seems to be to simultaneously hold those who have committed sex crimes accountable for their actions, understand the serious and devastating effect of those crimes on victims, and acknowledge that there are problems with the way we categorize and treat offenders, especially the way their situation is compounded with post-release punishment.

The problem of neighbors, of course, is boundless, ever-expanding, from the bugs in our gut to the so-far silent ETs and SETI searches. What could be more local, or more global? In my neighborhood I have almost a hundred neighbors crammed two-by-two into cinderblock cubicles, all of us pedophiles, rapists, or some other kind of sex offender. The larger facility is filled with people who hate sex offenders, spurred on by their own powerlessness or, sometimes, almost overwhelmed by the power that has been placed in their hands. It's a web of knots too tangled to untie, but it is also Indra's web, every node reflecting all others.

— *Henry*

TWENTY-NINE

May the Stars Remember

ONE SPRING EVENING AFTER rehearsal I stop at a roadside park to take a moment to collect my thoughts. It's already dark, and cold; my breath hangs in the air as I turn my eyes to the sky. The Milky Way magnifies itself overhead; standing beneath this sparkling vault, the night provokes a sense of awe in me. Space stretches into an immeasurable expanse, my life floating in the gap.

Podcast host Al Letson remarked after hearing a boys' chorus perform in a prison in Malawi: "(It was) the most beautiful sound I've ever heard. I'd never felt music that way before. I felt my broken heart begin to heal. Then it struck me—I am in the presence of God. I could feel something changing in my body—the universe was inside me, and I was connected to every piece of that universe, stars to person."[85]

The stars shine down on us, illuminating possibilities in the darkness of the night. We absorb that light, as it travels through our bodies, mingles with our molecules, and then perhaps radiates back out into the world through our voices.

Standing there, I remember the remarkable song Keith wrote.

Each season, Keith composed at least one song for the choir to perform. One of these—"May the Stars Remember Your Name"—soon took on an extraordinary life of its own. The song pays tribute to the value of being recognized and remembered when you're in a place where it's easy to be forgotten.

"I'd been locked up a couple years," Keith says, "and began remembering how things used to be. Spending time with friends, being able to see
the stars, sitting outside while my friends played guitar. I started to think
about not being able to see the stars for so long. Even at night the lights
inside are too bright. 'I haven't seen you for so long, but I remember; does
the same work for you, do you remember my name?'"

"The words started to flow. Eventually I got my poem—verse, chorus,
verse, chorus. I liked the meter, rhyme, and imagery. Everything I saw
in the poem told me the song needed to be a waltz, three-four time. In
my head I heard intervals. So I tried to relay that with notes. It was very
crude, mind you."

"Then Dr. Cohen worked her magic. She made small modifications to
the lyrics, and created a new melody. It stayed in three-four time, which
is something I'm proud of. I was in tune enough with my writing to feel
the meter."

Here's how the song goes:

*Once captive now I'm freed, once blind now I see, the beauty of the night
that's calling to me. Here I go, on my own, the cover of darkness to carry me
home. And the stars, and the stars remember, remember my name.*

*Between the sunrise, take a look deep inside, see a man that has changed,
while alone in the night.*

*Love shining bright, like stars in the night, answer the prayers that I send
out tonight.*

May the stars, may the stars, remember, remember your name.

The song became a highlight of our concerts that season. And after
those performances, it was picked up, through contacts Mary Cohen had,
by a Chicago dramatic advocacy organization, 'StoryCatchers Theater' at
Warrenville youth detention center, which allows young women to take
life stories and perform them as a play.

"The young women wrote a play about their mothers, and the play was
titled 'Mom in the Moon,'" Keith recalls. "They changed the words to
make my song fit the theme. It's really awesome how they worked it in."

This was all quite exciting enough, but here's where things get even
more interesting.

Perhaps you've heard of Yo-Yo Ma, the world's most virtuosic cellist? I
thought so. Ma had a three-year residency with the Chicago Symphony
Orchestra as creative consultant, and in that role he visited inmates at
Warrenville and performed for them with a small string ensemble. There
he encountered "May the Stars Remember Your Name," and liked it. Mary

Cohen was present and explained to Ma how the song came about. He made a few changes to it, and then he performed the song for the insiders at Warrenville.

Yo-Yo Ma played Keith's song!

"The whole experience was a shock," Keith says. "I knew who Yo-Yo Ma was before I was incarcerated. Just the fact that he played something I'd helped to write was enough to blow my mind. Add the fact that it happened while I was in prison, and it became a nuclear reaction."

"The choir was ecstatic; other inmates congratulated me, and my friends outside were flabbergasted. I feel I was humble about it. I didn't go around, 'Hey, I did this.' I don't believe the nature of the song and its journey really warranted that. I mailed a packet to the parole board that included newspaper articles about the song, but I don't know if it had any effect."

The funny thing is, Keith had been planning to attend a Yo-Yo Ma concert around the time of his arrest. Seven years later, he would get his wish. After Keith was released, in 2017, Ma happened to perform in Iowa City. Keith was thrilled to be able to attend the show.

I ran into him not long after, and he was all smiles. "It was a great show," he told me. The whole experience inspired Keith in many ways. "The confidence I have in my writing now," he says, "is enormous. That self-confidence may be the biggest asset I'll have back on the streets."

Take a look deep inside, see a man that has changed, while alone in the night. May the stars, may the stars, remember, remember your name.

THIRTY

Redemption Songs

INGING AT OAKDALE THE last few years, I've become interested in how a change of heart—the flowering of the seed of redemption—takes place for those who have committed crimes.

One dictionary defines redemption as: *regaining possession of something; clearing a debt.* Perhaps in this context it's about regaining or assuming one's basic humanity and sense of right and wrong, after paying, in some way, for the effect one's actions have had on society.

But such things, when they happen, don't happen overnight.

In 12 Step programs it's said, "It takes what it takes."

Greg Boyle writes, "The light bulb appears and it brightens. Who can explain how or when?" In his book, Boyle talks about employing young men who flout the rules. "We see in them what they don't see in themselves. Until they do." [86]

He describes visiting a gang member in prison, who asks him how many 'homies' he has buried, as a result of gang warfare.

'Seventy-five,' Boyle replies.

'Damn,' says the young man, 'when's it gonna end?'

'Mijo, it will end the minute you decide.'

'Well, then, I decide.'

Stories like these remind us that it's the power of acceptance of who and where one is in life, combined with an acknowledgment of our misdeeds, and the will to move forward, that can allow for change to take place, over time.

Outside or inside the fences, I think many of us wrestle with questions of redemption; we try to regain lost parts of ourselves, parts that have been squelched through traumatic experiences. And we try to square things with those we have hurt, repaying the debt of human feeling. This happens in an ongoing way; it's not a fixed-end process. As Mary Roche reminds us, if you truly want to come to terms with what you've done, you can't skip the stage of acknowledging that your actions have harmed others, and working to atone for them.

Achieving justice thus means offering a chance for accountability, healing, and restoration, for all involved, including the victim, in an engaged and inclusive process that builds from the foundation of a community up. Unfortunately, victim reparation, or some kind of framework that allows for an act of atonement to take place between offender and victim, is still limited in most places.

Forgiveness—of oneself and of others—isn't easy, but it's better for you in the long run. Baz Dreisinger describes a study in which participants were asked to recall a specific offending event and engage in four types of imagery: focusing on the hurt, nursing a grudge, empathizing with the offender's human qualities, or forgiving. The subjects who forgave manifested physiological changes such as lower blood pressure and lower heart rate.[87]

It seems axiomatic that personal change comes from within; people have to reach a point of wanting to be better. But people also need opportunities. A sense of hope. Second chances. It's like riding a bicycle—to keep your balance you have to continue to move forward, on smooth ground, or you fall. The opportunities offered by a caring community—embodying the concept of *ubuntu*, that we are who we are because of all of us together— can be part of these second chances.

It might seem odd to describe a prison as a caring community. But if we hope to break the chain of criminal thinking, then that's exactly the kind of environment we want prisons to be. And in that respect, in creating a sense of hope, the Oakdale Choir is cutting edge. It represents a tool for breaking through the sense of separation that plagues the criminal justice system.

Artist Rachel Rosenthal writes, "Working collaboratively centers you in the moment. This is one of the hardest things to do, since we live in a world that is so divisive and scattered and distracting, pulling us in every direction. This kind of work obliges you to surf the moment, to be in sync with the moment. And that is profoundly important for spiritual and psychological health."[88]

Maybe working together helps us transcend our individual flaws. Or, maybe, as we accept each other's flaws, they lose some of their power over us. It's like pouring water from different sources into one container, mingling the essences of each into the whole. We do this repeatedly, until after some time we begin to experience deeper waters, deeper layers of our humanity and an expanded sense of who we are.

Engagement in pro-social activity, creative expression, the modeling of positive emotions, retraining of the brain as suggested by the idea of neuroplasticity, developing resilience, all of these things can help anyone who sings in a choir, or engages in other creative work, to grow.

For many of the insiders encountered in this book, it's not been easy going beyond what they used to be. Many have experienced a measure of personal growth, but it can be a messy, one-step-forward, two-steps-back process. A commitment to something greater than themselves seems to have been crucial.

As Tennessee Williams put it, "Hell (can be) yourself and the only redemption is when a person puts himself aside to feel deeply for another person."

If a change of heart is needed in order to transition back into the world of useful citizenship, so, too, are practical skills: a basic education, job skills, and a post-release plan.

Patrick has been a bit pessimistic on this count: *To the state, rehabilitation means treatment: drug treatment, sex offender treatment, victim impact or abusive behavior and anger management. Not education. Not job training. Not certification courses. GED courses are mandated by the state of Iowa and that's it. Although some (few) institutions maintain a library of job search guides, almost nothing else is offered.*

All the other classes offered are taught or run by volunteers. In Oakdale: the choir, songwriter's workshop, writer's workshop, the job club, consumer economics, communication skills, civics, etc. Here [in the treatment facility he has been transferred to] *there is nothing. Only treatment.*

The felons most likely to reoffend are those with drug-related crimes. Since they are probably coming back, they are put through a 'treat-and-release' program that pushes them through the system and back onto the street, while doing nothing to provide alternatives to highly profitable drug dealing. 'Correctional' officers often joke with these inmates, volunteering to hold a bunk open for them on their next visit. Kind of like Motel 6 ... "We'll leave the light on for ya!" I know several inmates who have been locked up five or more times in the last 15 years.

What inmates need is education (beyond GED level), job skills, mentors when released, places to go and actual jobs where they can work and earn a living wage.

Patrick's pessimism is not misplaced. Many prisons offer little in the way of education and job training. Many prison programs were slashed nationally in the '80s and '90s. However, educational efforts do chug along at some prisons. One hour down the road from Iowa City, Grinnell College instructors teach courses at Newton Correctional Facility as part of a First Year of College Program. Such programs are inexpensive to run; you don't have to house or feed students, just pay the faculty.

There are other successes. An inmate who began taking classes in the Iowa State University Landscape Architecture program is now teaching the course for insiders. There's an apprenticeship program in horticulture at the women's prison in Mitchellville.

Scott Koepke, organic food and gardening educator, has planted a thriving vegetable garden at Oakdale with the help of insiders.

When it comes to prison music programs, Mary Cohen is keeping an eye on the numbers across the country, and they're growing. Prominent prison choirs include the East Hill Singers in Kansas, Umoja at the Lebanon Correctional Facility in Ohio, Ubuntu and Hope thru Harmony in Ohio, the Empowering Song program in Massachusetts, other choirs in Florida and Ohio, and Voices of Hope at Shakopee Women's Facility in Minnesota.[89] Cohen regularly receives emails from people interested in starting new ones.

Another exciting development at Oakdale is the nascent Liberal Arts Beyond Bars (LABB) program, spearheaded by Kathrina Litchfield at the University of Iowa Center for Human Rights. University faculty members are beginning to teach college classes on a variety of subjects, offering college credit to Oakdale inmates. For many, this is their first exposure to higher education. The program has also helped create greater access to internet resources for people in prison, using managed firewalls, so that only certain sites are accessible.[90]

As part of LABB, inside OCC singers became eligible to sign up for college credit for being part of the choir. To earn this credit, they have to submit written assignments and attend rehearsals faithfully. At the time of this writing, things are still in the experimental stage, but there's great enthusiasm among insiders. The size of the choir swells. The LABB website details the motivations for the program: "Research has shown that higher education programs in prisons can significantly reduce recidivism. While this is an important benefit, college-in-prison programs provide many more benefits. Our project aims to provide opportunities that broaden horizons, develop students' agency and increased civic engagement, encourage social change from the inside out, strengthen bonds with families and communities, break family legacies of incarceration, inspire inquiry and transformation, and create pathways for successful reentry with dignity and compassion. We aim to create an infrastructure that can soon sustain accredited college coursework toward a degree." Prison educators affirm that those who've been excluded from many of society's opportunities often become the most talented and engaged students. Some of the best teaching and learning happens in prison.

The choir continues to expand and grow and surprise everyone who comes into contact with it. Exciting things are happening. There are many more highlights than I could elaborate on in this book. A few of these include:

*Singing Melanie DeMore's song "Lead With Love," which, like many other songs, could serve as an anthem for the choir: *You got to put one foot in front of the other, and lead with love.*[91]

DeMore lives on the West Coast and is part of a grassroots movement called Community Sing, which is galvanizing its own energy around the practice of singing in the oral tradition (without the use of sheet music). A vibrant Community Sing group coalesces in Iowa City, and this becomes another focus in my life. There's an awareness within this movement that humans have always sung together to tell their stories, share joy and grief, and pass on culture like a flame.

Several people from the local Community Sing group volunteer with the OCC, and new songs written in one place migrate to the other, in a dynamic cross-fertilization. In this sense, the Oakdale choir is part of a broader renaissance—a growing movement of singing as a way to create community and cultivate soul. Other well-known Community Sing leaders, like Maggie Wheeler and Sara Thomsen, also visit the OCC and lead songs.

*Documentary filmmaker Daniel Kolen, son of choir member Amy, begins directing and producing a documentary film about the Oakdale choir, called *The Inside Singers*, which may be released soon.[92]

*The Soweto Gospel Choir from South Africa, in town for a concert, visits Oakdale and shares songs with the OCC, performing at one of our concerts and stopping just short of blowing the roof beams off the prison with their musical energy.

*OCC outsiders participate in a restorative justice listening session with crime victims and relatives, including four parents of murdered children. They listen as the parents share the impact these crimes had on them, the complex emotional processes they're going through. An idea is floated for coordinating a victim impact panel to speak at a songwriting workshop and at choir practice.

*And, in the spring of 2018, representatives of the Heartbeat Opera Company of New York City get in touch with Mary Cohen. They're presenting a modernized version of Beethoven's opera *Fidelio*.[93] Set in a prison, the opera features a 'prisoner's chorus.' The company's directors reach out to conductors of six Midwestern prison choirs, including Cohen, and ask them to learn a section of this chorus. They then travel to each of these prisons and videotape the choirs performing their section. The performances are also professionally audio-recorded.

In May of 2018 Heartbeat premieres the opera in New York City, and images of the six choirs are projected onto the scrim of the stage. The six segments are spliced together to form one cohesive song, which plays while the particular scene unfolds.

Mary Cohen was able to attend the premiere and later tells us it was incredibly moving. On top of this, media coverage of the OCC rehearsing the prisoner's chorus is picked up by CNN, and one on-line video of this rehearsal receives over 100,000 views.

Amidst all of these big moments, the choir members try and stay focused. We've got work to do.

In my dream tonight, a man languishes inside a large glass jar. A butterfly flits around him, banging against the glass. The man seems to be waiting to turn into a butterfly himself. Outside the jar it's snowing, cold, and there's a hard rock concert going on, with long-haired concert-goers clustered around the band.

I'm struck by these images and turn them over in my mind for a few days. A friend suggests this interpretation:

Butterflies are all about change. Snow and cold can mean locked-up or repressed emotion, in contrast to hard-rock music, which is a very dramatic, raw kind of emotional expression. The rock fans on the outside of the jar seem to be people who express themselves, who don't bottle up their emotions, who are somewhat free, despite the chilling effect of their environment.

What strikes me most, though, is the potential for the man's transformation. He waits for the day when despite everything, he too will turn into a butterfly, and fly away.

THIRTY-ONE

Dear Younger Me

I GET A PHONE CALL from Roger, the former Mennonite minister who has been in the OCC for several years, telling me that Patrick has been released from prison, and is living in the area. The local Mennonite Church helped find him a place to live. He shares a small home with another former Oakdale inmate, goes regularly to Mt. Pleasant for group work, and to the University hospitals for health care.

Roger passes along Patrick's phone number, and the next morning I give him a call. I feel strange dialing the number. For a while now I've communicated with him only through letters.

The phone rings, and I hear a familiar gravelly voice on the other end. "Hello?"

He's enjoying being out, but all the health issues of the past few years have come to a head. He's been diagnosed with cancer, and will begin chemo soon. I can't help but think of the poor diet, the stress of being inside, and the medical misdiagnoses he's written about, as contributing factors.

"Can I come visit you?"

"That would be real nice," he says.

I ask if there's anything I can bring him.

"I like crime novels."

Of course he does.

I find a copy of one of Lee Child's latest books—in the Jack Reacher series—and a few days later I drive out to a small town not far from Iowa

City. It's a beautiful drive. As I pass through one town, I see the community's effort to distinguish itself, as so many small Midwestern towns try to do: a large Star Trek USS Enterprise model on a prominent corner marks the "future birthplace of Capt. James T. Kirk."

I wind my way through and out of town and on to a gravel road. Corn and soybean fields stretch away from the road to the horizon. The residence is ahead on the right. A few tomato and pepper plants sprout in containers on the porch.

I knock. Patrick answers.

"Hey, there." We embrace. He shows me his room, nicely appointed with posters and placards, and maps of Biblical events. In the living room is a small aquarium, stocked with a few tropical fish. On shelves all the way around the kitchen, he points out his new collection of Coca Cola memorabilia—glasses, cans, and clocks. I guess it makes sense that he'd want to amass some material stuff. His collecting options have, until recently, been pretty limited.

We head into town to have lunch at a Chinese restaurant, where he orders the sesame chicken. Though he's had a colostomy bag installed, he has a good appetite. We talk about likes and dislikes now that he's out. He's following "Sons of Anarchy," a TV show about one of his former fascinations, outlaw bikers.

As we talk, he recalls his first fight. It was in 7th grade. A boy had been picking on him for months. Finally, Patrick let him have it. He spent a lot of time outside the principal's office that year, he says.

But he's been doing well post-release, apart from his health. He was given the privilege of internet use after just seven months. And he's no longer wearing an ankle bracelet. Both of these exceptions are unusual. His stepdaughter's support has been extremely helpful, he says.

Patrick asks me to drive him to the Goodwill reboot store, so he can pick up a used computer. He picks out a few matchable PC components for around $100. Then he wants to go to the "Stuff Etc." store to look for glasses to add to his Coke collection.

On our drive back home, he opens up about his rehabilitation. "How do you tell whether someone's sincere in his commitment to change?" he asks. "If they commit and keep showing up. If they'll look you in the eye. If they don't minimize their crime—'Oh, it was the drugs,' or, 'It wasn't that bad, that other guy was worse.' If they own their crime, not hemming and hawing when talking about it."

In his letters, Patrick claimed he was innocent of the sex abuse charge. Do I believe this? Do I trust him? I think so. Of course, I can't be certain, and when dealing with someone who has spent half his life on the other side of the law, it can be hard for trust to take hold. But I do think he has changed. He seems to be owning the fact that his life used to be off the rails. He's expressing the sense that he has come through the prison experience and is a different person.

He tells me he'd like to start a halfway house; he wants to work with sex offenders. They're considered the lepers of modern society, he says, the lowest of the low, and they need a lot of help.

But he's not sure how much time he has.

Prison activist Maya Schenwar writes, "We see prison as a solution to the problem of crime. Instead of preventing crime by allocating resources for healthcare, early childhood education, food, housing, and other basic needs, we're sending people to prison." [94] While research shows that strong communities can promote public safety and reduce crime, high rates of incarceration are tearing poor communities apart.

Schenwar goes so far as to suggest that ultimately prisons themselves ought to be done away with, that our society should explore other options for dealing with crime. It's a bold proposal. Tossing inmates into a confounding environment means they often become ever more entangled in criminal behavior, creating a series of knots seemingly impossible to unsnarl. Some studies do show that imprisonment actually increases crime. "Few people stop committing crimes because prison exists," researcher Todd Clear writes. "Prisons are schools of crime, returning people to the community further criminalized." [95]

If this is the case, then we're shelling out for our justice coming and going—our taxes pay for the not insignificant costs of housing and feeding the convicted (a year in prison can cost more than a year at Harvard), and we pay again when new crimes are committed by those who have been traumatized and criminalized by the prison experience and are released back into society.

I do think that prisons like Oakdale, run by enlightened wardens, and offering numerous volunteer-led programs for insiders, are bucking the trend. And reforms, such as more humane visiting policies, better healthcare, and less expensive phone calls, could help make prison a more restorative experience. But simply reforming prisons won't necessarily stop what happens to many when they're locked up. They and their family's lives are often damaged for good.

If our goal is not retribution, but restoration and wholeness, on all sides of the criminal justice equation, it only makes sense to invest, not only more money, but more time and energy and concern, into things like drug treatment, education, housing, counseling and jobs, out in the society, before outsiders become insiders. And to consider, for some, alternatives to incarceration, such as mental health courts, drug courts, community supervision, anger management programs, or halfway houses.

People released from prison or who are on parole face a whole new set of challenges, including difficulty in finding housing, jobs and other services. Most job applications ask you to check a box if you have a felony conviction, and many employers will throw out the application when they see that box checked. A prison sentence leaves a gap in your resumé that's hard to explain. There is, encouragingly, a movement to 'ban the box.' By 2016, 24 states and more than 150 cities and counties had done so, and some large corporations had joined them.[96]

Parolees are also not allowed to have contact with others on parole. But if people close to you have convictions, it can be hard to maintain ties of family or friendship, ties which could ordinarily help you to stay clean.

Finally, only thirty-eight states restore voting rights to felons after completion of sentence. Iowa and eight other states do not, relying on the pleasure of the governor or courts for restoration of such rights. [97]This is another layer of procedural prejudice.

After a few months, I get another call from Roger. Patrick is in the hospital, and not doing well. Perhaps now would be a good time to visit. A few days later I drive to the university hospital campus, park my car in the cavernous ramp, trek through the halls and with some difficulty find Patrick's room. His housemate, H, another former inmate, is there visiting.

Patrick looks gaunt. We talk about the prognosis. The cancer has spread, but he's hopeful he can go to a rehab center in Cedar Rapids to deal with a leg problem.

He tells me he needs to rest his eyes for a bit, so for a few minutes H and I talk about volunteerism. Lots of insiders at Oakdale are volunteers, too, H says, from hospice workers to organizers of charitable events.

"I was always a taker," H tells me. "Finally, I learned to be a giver." He's working on a book about this, he says.

Patrick has told me how much his friendship with H means to him. They understand each other, get what the other person is going through. Having someone to talk to on a daily basis has been a lifesaver.

Patrick has been dozing. He stirs.

"Can I offer a blessing?" I ask him.

"Sure," he says.

In order to share some positive energy with Patrick, I brought along a book of blessings by my current favorite poet, John O'Donohue. Flipping through the book, I pick one out, and begin to read.

May you have the commitment to harvest your life,

To heal what has hurt you, to allow it to come closer to you and become one with you.

May you have great dignity, may you have a sense of how free you are.

And above all may you be given the wonderful gift of meeting the eternal light and beauty that is within you.

It's time to go. There's a lot I want to say, thinking back on our time together in the choir, but I don't. Instead, gripping Patrick's hand, I say goodbye.

A month later, the news comes: Patrick has passed.

The funeral will be held at the church in Kalona he attended. I drive down to attend. It's a fundamentalist Mennonite church, the men wearing straw hats, checkered shirts and overalls, and the women in plain dresses. These Mennonites, I've heard, have committed themselves to supporting returning citizens, no matter their crime. I'm happy to see that a contingent of the Oakdale choir have shown up to sing.

The service bulletin notes highlights from Patrick's life: "From a young age he was in love with singing. He performed with several choirs and started a Christian rock band called Seraph. In addition to being a talented singer, Patrick was also incredibly intelligent and very gifted at writing. His songs and poems have touched many hearts and he has impacted many lives. His life was interesting and complicated and he made countless poor life decisions."

The pastor stands to offer a few remarks on Patrick's journey, emphasizing the importance faith played in his later years. He turns to Matthew 20, a Bible verse likening the kingdom of heaven to a situation in which a landowner goes out early in the morning to hire workers for his vineyard. This landowner continues to hire people throughout the day, even late into the afternoon. At the end of the day, all the workers are paid the same amount. There's some grumbling.

The landlord says, 'I am not being unfair to you, friend. Didn't you agree to work for a denarius? Take your pay and go. I want to give the one who was hired last the same as I gave you.'

I'm sure most of the farmers in striped shirts clutching their straw hats believe that Patrick is now in heaven. My own complicated relationship with Christianity leaves me leaning away from the idea of heaven. Sitting among these good people, and thinking about the journey of the last few years, and the sense of community I've found in the choir, I find myself needing to take a broader view of this "kingdom of heaven," to focus on what it might mean here and now.

One interpretation might be that it's a place of peace within oneself, where inner turmoil is reconciled, and joy rises untroubled. Another might be that it's any place where justice prevails, and people treat each other with respect. A true community. Perhaps it represents an ongoing commitment to living fully, using one's whole potential, and creating a society where everyone can do the same. Restorative justice would fit this picture. The concept of redemption would, too. In such a vision, would not the last be first, and the first last?

Those who have committed crimes and been incarcerated are, in a sense, coming late to the work of contributing as a mature and productive member of society. Can we as a society let go of our grumbling and offer them what all people want—a chance to thrive?

Patrick's roommate also speaks, brushing away tears, talking about how he and Patrick supported each other in small ways, about how good it had been to have a companion who understood the challenges of life post-prison.

The ten or so members of the OCC rise now, all of them friends with, or at least familiar with, Patrick. Their voices ring out in the small church. People close their eyes and listen, some of them shedding tears, as the choir delivers a moving rendition of Patrick's song, "Dear Younger Me."

Afterwards, the church ladies lay out a spread of casseroles and desserts. I don't stay for the dinner, but get back in my car and drive to Iowa City, along country roads lined by fields of yellowing corn. The lyrics of "Dear Younger Me" ring in my ears.

Dear younger me, I've finally made it through as you can see, So now I'll pass on back to you the things I think will get us through, Cause we only get one chance at life's dance, Yes, we only get one chance at life's dance.

Careful who you trust, let some pass by if you must, better to slow down and wait, than let some nut control your fate. Seek out good advice, it may not always seem so nice, but others walked where you are now. Their wisdom just might help somehow.

Keep and seek your dreams, I know it's harder than it seems, find someone to lend a hand, and when you're right, then take a stand. Admit to your mistakes, you're sometimes wrong, it's just the breaks, find the place where you belong, what doesn't kill you, only makes you strong.

Believe in your self worth, there's none more worthy on this earth, don't let the hurdles that you face, throw you off or slow your pace. Strive to keep your word, let slurs and insults stay unheard, don't hesitate to compliment, communicate your real intent.

The truth is always best, even when you feel hard-pressed, ask for help when you need it most, no matter what you've got, don't boast. Always claim your blame, don't unload on someone's name. Send hatred quickly on its way, it kills you if you let it stay.

In the end you will see, it can be better for you than it was for me.

THIRTY-TWO

A Change is Gonna Come

A WARM BREEZE IS BLOWING up from the south, as pink buds appear on the crabapple trees outside the prison. It's concert day again.

Insiders arrive at the gym early in order to deal with logistics. They set up rows of chairs, roll in the piano, and those with a technological bent unspool the wires for the sound system and do sound checks.

Armand has been planning a speech. He wanders in, distracted, going over some notes he's been revising. Soon, the outside choir members file in to the gym and greet the insiders, milling around until Mary calls for our attention.

She climbs onto the podium, wearing her purple "Love Lives On" T-shirt with the Oakdale Community Choir logo across the back, the same shirt we are all wearing—purple for outsiders, green for insiders.

She has a message for us: "I want to congratulate you all on the progress you've made this past year. In terms of the choir's overall blended sound, you've made great strides!" We nod, smiling. Yep, that's us, well-blended in more ways than one. A few people exchange high fives.

Meanwhile, concert guests are navigating the protocol to enter the prison, passing through the metal detector, and clipping on their temporary badges, having been briefed on what to wear and how to behave.

In the free moments before the concert begins I strike up a conversation with a middle-aged white man named Trent. On the outside, he was an accountant. As an inmate, he says, he's working with a recovery group that combines the 12 steps of AA with the eight points of the Beatitudes.

"You get real with yourself, with what you've done," in this program, he tells me. "You can look in the mirror and see who you really are." The group addresses all kinds of addictions—drugs, alcohol, sex. He wants to continue to work with it after he's released.

"Addiction is just a way of filling a hole in yourself," he tells me. "You may stop drinking because you got married, but then fall into overeating. You have to have a healthy approach."

As we rejoin our sections and watch the visitors file in, I think about the parents and relatives attending this concert, who afterwards will get to visit their sons or husbands or brothers for a few moments. Many of these visitors will be recognized and introduced to the audience by their insider connections during the concert. These inside singers are visibly excited; you can see how much the visit means to them.

I wonder what the parents might be feeling. Shame that their son is in prison? Pride that they're doing all right, that they're engaged and involved in things like singing in the choir? Probably it's a complicated mix of emotions.

Time to begin. A hush falls over the gymnasium. Mary raises her hands and brings us in on the first song. We open, as usual, with "Beauty Before Me," but this time the choir starts out singing in a structured way, then slowly dissolves into free-form singing, improvising as we have done in numerous rehearsals throughout the year, building on what we've been learning, the notes ringing out in the way each singer discerns the need to sing them.

Armand looks up at the chart hanging from Mary's podium listing the order of the concert. He takes a deep breath. His moment will not happen until near the end of the concert.

We search in our folders for "Homeward Bound" and Amy takes the mic: "This song talks of physical and spiritual journeys, of growth and change. We should all be free to choose where we propel our positive energies. Think of the relationship between parents and children. If we're allowed to discover what we want to do in this life and who we want to be, we'll come back to those who loved us enough to allow us to live our own lives, and trusted that we would return."

The piano opens plaintively, the women's high voices set the mood, and the men respond.

In the quiet misty morning, when the moon has gone to bed. If you find it's me you're missing, if you're hoping I'll return, to your thought I'll soon be listening, in the road I'll stop and turn.

It's a gorgeous, poignant song, and might spur the reflective listener to ask, when am I given moments in my life to stop, turn, and listen?

"We are the Ones" has been a challenge for us this season. It's a song written by 'Sweet Honey in the Rock's' Bernice Johnson Reagon, reflecting the struggle to change the pass laws in South Africa, but it's not easy. But today it coalesces, as our voices construct a scaffolding of sound. The basses create a deep foundation of rhythm, a pulsing beat that drives the song forward, and each group of voices adds another layer above them.

We are the ones, we are the ones, we are the ones we been waiting for.

"I Wish that I Could Show You," "Watching Over Me," "How Can I Keep from Singing?"—with each song the momentum of the concert builds. The audience seems to feel it, too, reacting with increasing fervor and appreciation.

One of the insiders now steps up to the mic. "'People Get Ready' is about preparing for a new way of life," he says. "Getting ready to live outside these walls, trying to live each day with love and peace as if it were my last. I'm working on my family relationships—I want my wife and daughter to be able to trust and feel safe with me. So I'm taking some classes to learn about the only thing I can control, my attitude about myself and others and how I respond to situations. My goal for the future is to build on controlling anger, getting a job, returning to loved ones, and becoming a productive person in community. I hope some day I can use my own positive actions to influence others. So, people get ready."

There's laughter and clapping as we launch into the song, a beautiful soul hit which concludes with us harmonizing on the line, "I'm getting ready, I'm getting ready, This time I'm ready, this time I'm ready."

Listening to the sentiments expressed in both the introductions and the songs, I remember what another volunteer told me recently. An insider said to her, 'I used to not be a very nice person. But I'm different now.'

This reminds me that what we call things invests them with power. I've become more conscious about how I refer to people in the choir. Inmate, convict, or offender—such words define people by the worst thing they've ever done, and don't imply the possibility of change. 'Person in prison,' 'insider,' 'returning citizen,' these convey a different sense. Or how about 'inside artist, writer or musician?'

There are two main narratives people seem to hold in relation to the imprisoned. The first is that most people in prison are dangerous criminals, hardened to human feeling, unforgivable. The other is that people in prison are flawed human beings, trying to figure out how to better themselves, atone for their crimes and move forward with their lives.

Obviously, there's a kernel of truth in both narratives. Violent people do exist inside, though I believe that even the most hardened can change. And men and women who have come to a point of actively seeking redemption in their lives are in prison as well. There are two wolves living in each person, the Cherokee saying goes; one resentful, and one generous. Which wolf wins?

The one you feed.

I think back to Mary Cohen's research questions. Can typical inmate behaviors—the need for instant gratification, a lack of personal and social responsibility, and weakly developed social skills—be addressed, even modified to some degree, through the discipline of singing in a choir? I think the answer has become clear.

Human beings have a fundamental need to experience personal power and autonomy. If a person is causing harm because they're not feeling powerful, then taking more power away from them isn't going to be helpful. The solution may be to help them experience power—give them a voice—in a way that doesn't take away someone else's power.

I'm pulled from my reverie as Armand steps to the mic, the process of preparation these last few days buzzing through his being. He's nervous, but ready.

"Being locked up," he begins, gazing out at the crowd, "you find out who is with you and who isn't. When you're out and running free you may think you have a lot of friends."

"But in here you find out it's all about family at the end of the day. I'm thinking about my sister; and my family who has stuck with me. Well, I run into beautiful sisters and brothers here inside, too." He flashes a grin at the choir, and holds his hand out toward us.

"What kind of drugs are these people on? What would make you want to come in with a group of felons, and treat us like one big family? And Dr. Cohen, who do you think you are, telling me I'm a superstar? When others said I was unfit. Is this some kind of joke? Folks don't act like this in real life. Don't you know you're standing next to criminals?"

He turns and addresses the choir directly. "You're my sisters and brothers."

With his moment of honest humor, Armand has punctured some stereotypical assumptions, just as he's done with the songs he's written all along, like "So Much More," and come to think of it, with his other writing, too, like the advice column. He's to be transferred soon, moving on, and I know this is on his mind. For the moment, though, he's connecting with everyone in the gym. The audience is laughing and we're all grinning wildly.

Smiling, Armand sits down. Another man, a middle-aged white insider, comes to the front to introduce our last song.

"'A Change is Gonna Come' reminds me of my own journey," he stands before the microphone and says. "It seems I've been running all my life. Running from authority, from relationships, and from my own mistakes. There've been many changes in my life and I know there will be more. Though the past has been dark, I've developed new ways of thinking to challenge old patterns."

Mary steps up, and as usual, encourages us to smile. As the Sam Cooke lyrics begin to fill the gymnasium, the audience perks up in nostalgic recognition.

It's been a long, a long time coming
But I know a change is gonna come, oh yes it will.

A trombone rings out above our voices, brass tones swelling the air in the gymnasium and echoing off the ceiling.

The soloist lifts his voice in hopeful melodic flow, then brings the song home with soulful aplomb. As we come to the end, the audience erupts in wild applause. We look around at each other, basking in the love. I catch Terence's eye and he smiles. It was a pretty good performance, not without its flaws, but we're all pretty happy.

Some of the men set out juice and cookies, always a big draw, and we step out into the crowd.

ACKNOWLEDGEMENTS

I want to offer heartfelt thanks to Margaret Koenig, Heal McKnight, Cecile Goding, Eric Jones, Steve Locher and Mary Cohen for reading and commenting on drafts of this book. And hearty thanks to my writing group—Tim Bascom, Cecile Goding, Amy Kolen, Lois Cole and Eric Jones—for their ever-present wisdom and support. I'm grateful to the men in prison who shared their stories with me. Thanks, also, to members of the Victim Advisory Council for providing perspective on the finished manuscript. And thanks to Robin Hemley for planting the seed for this book.

The events depicted in this book mostly took place during the years 2012-2014, although some later highlights have been included. Several years of the choir's existence have been conflated into one year in order to create a smooth narrative flow, and some license was taken in terms of which songs were performed in which season.

Although I consider insiders and outsiders to be equal members of the choir, I have changed the names of inside singers, so as to be respectful of the rights of victims who might not want to see the actual names of offenders in print.

Book design is by Cheryl Totty at www.logicalinks.com. Copyediting is by Steven Richheimer. Author photo by Gabriel K Havel-Sturdevant. Layout by Devashish Donald Acosta.

ENDNOTES

1.   This description of Oakdale is based on personal correspondence with Patrick, and: Josh O'Leary, "Inside Oakdale", *Iowa City Press-Citizen* (August 3, 2013).

2.   Shrii Shrii Anandamurti, "Dogma – No more", *Neohumanism in a Nutshell, Part 1* (Calcutta: Ananda Marga Pracaraka Samgha, 1987).

3.   https://oakdalechoir.lib.uiowa.edu

4.   Adam Gopnik, "The Caging of America", *The New Yorker* (January 30, 2012).

5.   Adam Gopnik, "The Caging of America", *The New Yorker* (January 30, 2012), and John Pfaff, "How We Misunderstand Mass Incarceration", *The New Yorker* (April 10, 2017).

6.   Oliver Roeder, Lauren-Brooke Eisen and Julia Bowling, "What Caused the Crime Decline?"(New York University Brennan Center for Justice, 2015).

7.   Robert Perkinson, *Texas Tough: The Rise of America's Prison Empire* (New York: Picador, 2010) 11.

8.   Lawrence Friedman, *Crime and Punishment in American History* (New York: Basic Books, 1994) 404.

9.   James Surowiecki, "A Trump Bonanza for Private Prisons", *The New Yorker* (December 5, 2016).

10.   Adam Gopnik, "The Caging of America", *The New Yorker* (January 30, 2012).

11.   Edith Turner, *The Anthropology of Collective Joy* (New York: Palgrave Macmillan US, 2012).

12.   https://www.en.wikipedia.org/wiki/Vedran_Smallovic

13.   Ana Hernandez, *The Sacred Art of Chant* (Nashville, TN: Skylight Paths Publishing, 2005).

14.   Richard Williams, "Back from the Brink," *The Guardian*, (July 21, 2000).

15. Oliver Sacks, *An Anthropologist on Mars* (New York: Alfred A Knopf, 1995).

16. Alan Lomax, "Murderers' Home" (Pye Nixa label, 1957), and 'Negro Prison Songs' (Tradition label, 1958). http://deathisnot.bandcamp.com.

17. https://sunrecords.com

18. https://www.bbc.com/news/magazine-21084323

19. https://www.ted.com/speakers/the_lady_lifers

20. https://www.shakespearebehindbars.org

21. Don Lee, "Finding Freedom Through Song", *The Voice*, (Spring 2014).

22. Cohen, M. L., "Explorations of inmate and volunteer choral experiences in a prison-based choir", *Australian Journal of Music Education* (2007).

23. Cohen, M. L., "Prison choirs: Studying a unique phenomenon", *Choral Journal*, 47-50 (November, 2007).

24. Cohen, M. L., *Christopher Small's concept of musicking: Toward a theory of choral singing pedagogy in prison contexts* (2007).

25. Bruce Kittle, "More to restorative justice than meets the eye", *Iowa City Press-Citizen* (April 29, 2016).

26. Buzz Alexander, *Teaching the Arts behind Bars,* Rachel Marie-Crane Williams, (Ed.) (Boston, MA: Northeastern Press, 2003) Xiii.

27. Cohen, M. L., "Select music programs and restorative practices in prisons across the US and the UK", *Harmonizing the diversity that is community music activity: Proceedings from the International Society of Music Education (ISME) 2010 Seminar of the Commission for Community Music Activity*, D. Coffman (Ed.) International Society for Music Education (2010).

28. Robert Johnson, "Art and Autonomy: Prison Writers under Siege," *The Arts of Imprisonment*, Leonidas K Cheliotis, (Ed.) (Farnham, UK: Ashgate Publishing, 2012) 168.

29. https://doc.iowa.gov/administration/prison-rape-elimination-act

30. Robert Erme, "Attention-Deficit/Hyperactivity Disorder and Correctional Health Care", *Journal of Correctional Health Care* 15 (1) (February, 2009).

31. https://www.prisonpolicy.org/reports/income.html

32. Lawrence Friedman, *Crime and Punishment in American History* (New York: Basic Books, 1994) 83.

33. John Gunn, "Criminal behaviour and mental disorders", *British Journal of Psychiatry 130* (1977).

34. https://data.iowa.gov/Public-Safety/What-are-the-most-common-offenses-committed-by-tho/3vdk-edb4

35. Bruce Kittle, "Restorative Justice and Faith Communities", Sixth Judicial District, Iowa Department of Correctional Services.

36. Daniel Bergner, God of the Rodeo: The Search for Hope, Faith, and a Six-Second Ride in Louisiana's Angola Prison (New York: Ballantine, 1998).

37. Don Lee, "Finding Freedom Through Song", *The Voice* (Spring, 2014).

38.   https://www.nij.gov/topics/corrections/recidivism/Pages/welcome.aspx

39.   https://www.prisonpolicy.org/reports/parole_grades_table.html

40.   Mary Cohen, "'Mother Theresa, how can I help you?' The story of Elvera Roth, Robert Shaw and the Bethel College Benefit Sing-Along for Arts in Prison, Inc.", *International Journal of Research in Choral Singing, 3 (1),* (2008).

41.   Lawrence Friedman, *Crime and Punishment in American History* (New York: Basic Books, 1994).

42.   Friedman, *Crime and Punishment in American History* (New York: Basic Books, 1994) 80.

43.   Robert Perkinson, *Texas Tough: The Rise of America's Prison Empire* (New York: Picador, 2010), 8.

44.   Catherine Wilson, "If You Listen, I'll Tell You How I Feel: Incarcerated Men Expressing Emotion Through Songwriting", PhD Thesis, Graduate College of The University of Iowa (December, 2013)..

45.   Laresse Harvey, "Creativity inside and outside prison walls: A journey of inspiration", *International Journal of Community Music* (March 2010).

46.   Cohen, Mary, and Duncan, Stuart Paul, *Silenced Voices: Music-making in Theory and in Practice* (not yet published).

47.   Ibid.

48.   ttps://www.kcet.org/shows/artbound/arts-in-corrections-program-returns-to-california-prisons

49.   Grady Hillman, "The Mythology of the Corrections Community", *Teaching the Arts Behind Bars*, Rachel Marie-Crane Williams (Ed.) (Boston, MA: Northeastern Press, 2003) 17.

50.   Don Sabo, Terry Kuper and Willie London, *Prison Masculinities*, (Temple University Press, 2001), in James Samuel Logan, *Good Punishment? Christian Moral Practice and US Imprisonment* (Wm. B. Eerdmans Publishing Company, 2008).

51.   Tracy Frisch, "Criminal Injustice: Maya Schenwar on the failure of mass incarceration", *The Sun* (June, 2015).

52.   Ibid.

53.   Adam Gopnik, "The Caging of America", *The New Yorker* (January 30, 2012).

54.   https://www.prisonpolicy.org/blog/2017/04/10/wages

55.   Jessica Benko, "The Strange and Radical Humaneness of Norway's Halden Prison", *New York Times Magazine* (May 26, 2015).

56.   Ibid.

57.   Ibid.

58.   Laura M. Maruschak, *BJS Statistician,* Marcus Berzofsky, Dr. P.H., and Jennifer Unangst, *RTI International,* "Medical Problems of State and Federal Prisoners and Jail Inmates", (US Department of Justice, 2011–12).

59.   https://www.legis.iowa.gov/docs/publications/SD/16260.pdf

60.   Jennifer Bronson and Marcus Berzofsky, "Indicators of Mental Health

Problems Reported by Prisoners and Jail Inmates" (U.S. Department of Justice Special Report, 2011-2012).

61.   Bryan Stevenson, *Just Mercy: A Story of Justice and Redemption* (New York: Spiegel and Grau, 2015).

62.   Rebecca Solnit, *The Encyclopedia of Trouble and Spaciousness* (San Antonio, TX: Trinity University Press, 2014) 228.

63.   http://www.treatmentadvocacycenter.org/browse-by-state/iowa

64.   Mary Cohen and Perry Miller, "'Dear Younger Me': Writing, songwriting and choral singing while incarcerated as a means to build identities and bridge communities." M. Reason (Ed.) *Elusive evidence: Documenting, measuring, and evaluating arts practice in social context* (in press)..

65.   James Q Whitman in James Samuel Logan, *Good Punishment? Christian Moral Practice and US Imprisonment* (Grand Rapids, MI: Wm. B. Eerdmans Publishing Company, 2008) 29.

66.   Daniel Karpowitz and Max Kenner, "Education as Crime Prevention: The Case for Reinstating Pell Grant Eligibility for the Incarcerated" (Bard Prison Initiative, 1995) https://www.prisonpolicy.org

67.   P R Sarkar, *A Few Problems Solved Part 6* (Calcutta: Ananda Marga Pracaraka Samgha, 1988).

68.   Greg Boyle, *Tattoos on the Heart: The Power of Boundless Compassion* (New York: Free Press, 2011) 190.

69.   https://www.forbes.com/sites/dianahembree/2018/05/22/ceo-pay-skyrockets-to-361-times-that-of-the-average-worker/#2c5699b7776d

70.   Mark Lewis Taylor, *The Executed God*, in James Samuel Logan, *Good Punishment? Christian Moral Practice and US Imprisonment* (Grand Rapids, MI: Wm. B. Eerdmans Publishing Company, 2008) 38.

71.   https://www.hrw.org/news/2016/10/12/us-disastrous-toll-criminalizing-drug-use.

72.   Michele Alexander, *The New Jim Crow: Mass Incarceration in the Age of Colorblindness* (New York: The New Press, 2012)..

73.   Ibid.

74.   Laura Edge, *Locked Up: A History of the US Prison System* (Minneapolis, MN: Twenty-first Century Books, 2009) 41.

75.   Elizabeth Hinton, *From the War on Poverty to the War on Crime: The Making of Mass Incarceration in America* (Boston, MA: Harvard University Press, 2017).

76.   Robert Perkinson, *Texas Tough: The Rise of America's Prison Empire* (New York: Picador, 2010).

77.   Tracy Frisch, "Criminal Injustice: Maya Schenwar on the failure of mass incarceration," *The Sun* (June 2015).

78.   https://onbeing.org/programs/richard-davidson-a-neuroscientist-on-love-and-learning-feb2019/#transcript

79.   Mary Cohen and Catherine Wilson, "Inside the fences: The processes

and purposes of songwriting in an adult male U.S. prison" *International Journal of Music Education* (2012).

80. John Pfaff, "How we misunderstand Mass Incarceration", *The New Yorker* (April 10, 2017).

81. https://www.afsc.org/resource/solitary-confinement-facts.

82. Martin Buber, *I and Thou* (Eastford, CT: Martino Publishing, 2010).

83. Georgia Harlem, "Sex Laws: Unjust and Ineffective," *The Economist* (Aug 6, 2009).

84. Ibid.

85. Al Letson, "The Possibilities of the Stars", State of the Re:Union podcast (January 8, 2014).

86. Greg Boyle, *Tattoos on the Heart: The Power of Boundless Compassion* (New York: Free Press, 2011) 110-111.

87. Baz Dreisinger, *Incarceration Nations: A Journey to Justice in Prisons Around the World* (New York: Other Press, 2017).

88. Rachel Rosenthal in Rachel Marie-Crane Williams, *Teaching the Arts behind Bars,* (Boston, MA: Northeastern Press, 2003) 146.

89. Cohen, M.L., and Henley, J. "Music-making behind bars: The many dimensions of community music in prisons". Submitted for publication in the Oxford Handbook of Community Music.

90. Kathrina Litchfield, director of Liberal Arts Beyond Bars, personal correspondence.

91. https://www.youtube.com/watch?v=9w22S8foSbk

92. https://www.indiegogo.com/projects/the-inside-singers-a-documentary#/

93. https://www.heartbeatopera.org/fidelio

94. Tracy Frisch, "Criminal Injustice: Maya Schenwar on the failure of mass incarceration", *The Sun* (June 2015).

95. https://www.pbs.org/wgbh/frontline/article/todd-clear-why-americas-mass-incarceration-experiment-failed

96. Frisch, "Criminal Injustice: Maya Schenwar on the failure of mass incarceration", *The Sun* (June 2015).

97. https://www.thoughtco.com/where-felons-can-and-cannot-vote-3367689

BIBLIOGRAPHY

Alexander, Michele, *The New Jim Crow: Mass Incarceration in the Age of Colorblindness* (New York: The New Press, 2012).

Anandamurti, "Dogma—No more", *Neohumanism in a Nutshell, Part 1* (Calcutta: Ananda Marga Pracaraka Samgha, 1987).

Benko, Jessica, "The Strange and Radical Humaneness of Norway's Halden Prison", *New York Times Magazine* (May 26, 2015).

Bergner, Daniel, *God of the Rodeo: The Search for Hope, Faith, and a Six-Second Ride in Louisiana's Angola Prison* (New York: Ballantine, 2011).

Boyle, Greg, *Tattoos on the Heart: The Power of Boundless Compassion* (New York: Free Press, 2011).

Bronson, Jennifer, and Berzofsky, Marcus, "Indicators of Mental Health Problems Reported by Prisoners and Jail Inmates" (U.S. Department of Justice Special Report, 2011-2012).

Buber, Martin, *I and Thou* (Eastford, CT: Martino Publishing, 2010).

Cheliotis, Leonidas K (Ed), *The Arts of Imprisonment*, (Farnham, UK: Ashgate Publishing, 2012).

Cohen, M. L. "Prison choirs: Studying a unique phenomenon", *Choral Journal* (November, 2007).

Cohen, M. L., "Explorations of inmate and volunteer choral experiences in a prison-based choir", *Australian Journal of Music Education, 1* (2007).

Cohen, M. L., *Christopher Small's concept of musicking: Toward a theory of choral singing pedagogy in prison contexts* (2007).

Cohen, M. L., "Select music programs and restorative practices in prisons across the US and the UK", *Harmonizing the diversity that is community music activity: Proceedings from the International Society of Music Education (ISME) 2010 Seminar of the Commission for Community Music Activity,*

D. Coffman (Ed.), International Society for Music Education (2010).

Cohen, Mary, "'Mother Theresa, how can I help you?' The story of Elvera Roth, Robert Shaw and the Bethel College Benefit Sing-Along for Arts in Prison, Inc." *International Journal of Research in Choral Singing, 3 (1)* (2008).

Cohen, Mary, *International Journal of Community Music* (March 2010).

Cohen, M.L. and Wilson, C. "Inside the fences: The processes and purposes of songwriting in an adult male U.S. prison." *International Journal of Music Education.* (2012).

Cohen, Mary and Miller, Perry, "'Dear Younger Me': Writing, songwriting and choral singing while incarcerated as a means to build identities and bridge communities." M. Reason (Ed.) *Elusive evidence: Documenting, measuring, and evaluating arts practice in social context.* (in press).

Cohen, Mary, and Duncan, Stuart Paul, *Silenced Voices: Music-making in Theory and in Practice* (not yet published).

Dreisinger, Baz, *Incarceration Nations: A Journey to Justice in Prisons Around the World* (New York: Other Press, 2017).

Edge, Laura, *Locked Up: A History of the US Prison System* (Minneapolis, MN: Twenty-first Century Books, 2009).

Friedman, Lawrence, *Crime and Punishment in American History* (New York: Basic Books, 1994).

Frisch, Tracy, "Criminal Injustice: Maya Schenwar on the failure of mass incarceration", *The Sun* (June 2015).

Gopnik, Adam, "The Caging of America", *The New Yorker* (Jan 30, 2012).

Gunn, John, "Criminal behaviour and mental disorders", *British Journal of Psychiatry 130* (1977).

Harlem, Georgia, "Sex Laws: Unjust and Ineffective," *The Economist* (Aug 6, 2009).

Harvey, Laresse, "Creativity inside and outside prison walls: A journey of inspiration", *International Journal of Community Music* (March 2010).

Hernandez, Ana, *The Sacred Art of Chant* (Nashville, TN: Skylight Paths Publishing, 2005).

Hinton, Elizabeth, *From the War on Poverty to the War on Crime: The Making of Mass Incarceration in America* (Boston, MA: Harvard University Press, 2017).

Johnson, Robert, "Art and Autonomy: Prison Writers under Siege ", *The Arts of Imprisonment*, Leonidas K Cheliotis, (Ed.) (Farnham, UK: Ashgate Publishing, 2012).

Karpowitz, Daniel, and Kenner, Max, "Education as Crime Prevention: The Case for Reinstating Pell Grant Eligibility for the Incarcerated" (Bard Prison Initiative, 1995).

Kittle, Bruce, "More to restorative justice than meets the eye", *Iowa City Press-Citizen* (April 29, 2016).

Kittle, Bruce, "Restorative Justice and Faith Communities", Sixth Judicial District, Iowa Department of Correctional Services.

Lee, Don, "Finding Freedom Through Song", *The Voice* (Spring, 2014).

Logan, James Samuel, *Good Punishment? Christian Moral Practice and US Imprisonment* (Grand Rapids, MI: Wm. B. Eerdmans Publishing Company, 2008).

Lozoff, Bo, *We're All Doing Time* (Durham, NC: Human Kindness Foundation, 1998).

Maruschak, Laura M., BJS Statistician, Berzofsky, Marcus, Dr., and Jennifer Unangst, RTI International, "Medical Problems of State and Federal Prisoners and Jail Inmates", (*U.S. Department of Justice* 2011–12).

McKay, Joyce, "Reforming Prisoners and Prisons: Iowa's State Prisons—The First Hundred Years", *The Annals of Iowa, State Historical Society of Iowa* (Vol. 60, no. 2).

O'Donohue, John, *Anam Cara* (New York: HarperCollins, 1997).

O'Leary, Josh, "Inside Oakdale", *Iowa City Press-Citizen* (August 3, 2013).

Perkinson, Robert, *Texas Tough: The Rise of America's Prison Empire* (New York: Picador, 2010).

Pfaff, John, "How We Misunderstand Mass Incarceration", *The New Yorker* (April 10, 2017).

Roeder, Oliver, Eisen, Lauren-Brooke, and Bowling, Julia, "What Caused the Crime Decline?" *NYU Brennan Center Brennan Center for Justice* (2015).

Sacks, Oliver, *An Anthropologist on Mars* (New York: Alfred A Knopf, 1995).

Sarkar, P. R., *A Few Problems Solved Part 6*, (Calcutta: Ananda Marga Pracaraka Samgha, 1988).

Schenwar, Maya, *Locked Down, Locked Out: Why Prison Doesn't Work and How We Can Do Better* (Oakland, CA: Berrett-Koehler Publishers, 2014).

Solnit, Rebecca, *The Encyclopedia of Trouble and Spaciousness* (San Antonio, TX: Trinity University Press, 2014).

Stevens, Wallace, "Esthetique du mal", *Selected Poems* (New York: Alfred A Knopf, 2009).

Stevenson, Bryan, *Just Mercy: A Story of Justice and Redemption* (New York: Spiegel and Grau, 2015).

Surowiecki, James, "A Trump Bonanza for Private Prisons", *The New Yorker* (December 5, 2016).

Turner, Edith, *The Anthropology of Collective Joy* (New York: Palgrave Macmillan US, 2012)

Williams, Rachel Marie-Crane, (Ed.), *Teaching the Arts behind Bars* (Boston, MA: Northeastern Press, 2003).

Williams, Richard, "Back from the Brink," *The Guardian* (July 21, 2000).

Wilson, Catherine, "If you listen, I'll tell you how I feel: Incarcerated men expressing emotion through songwriting", PhD Thesis, Graduate College of The University of Iowa (December 2013).

ONLINE SOURCES AND RESOURCES

Iowa Department of Corrections FY2012 Annual Report https://www.legis.iowa.gov/docs/publications/SD/16260.pdf

Cuddy, Amy, "Your body language may shape who you are", TED.com (Mar 11, 2014).

https://oakdalechoir.lib.uiowa.edu

https://en.wikipedia.org/wiki/Vedran_Smallovic

deathisnot.bandcamp.com.

https://www.ted.com/speakers/the_lady_lifers

https://www.shakespearebehindbars.org

https://www.prisonpolicy.org/global/

https://www.ncjrs.gov/App/abstractdb/AbstractDBDetails.aspx?id=252565

https://doc.iowa.gov/administration/prison-rape-elimination-act

https://data.iowa.gov/Public-Safety/What-are-the-most-common-offenses-committed-by-tho/3vdk-edb4

https://www.pbs.org/wgbh/frontline/article/todd-clear-why-americas-mass-incarceration-experiment-failed/

https://www.nij.gov/topics/corrections/recidivism/Pages/welcome.aspx

http://www.treatmentadvocacycenter.org/browse-by-state/iowa

https://www.forbes.com/sites/dianahembree/2018/05/22/ceo-pay-sky-rockets-to-361-times-that-of-the-average-worker/#2c5699b7776d

https://www.hrw.org/news/2016/10/12/us-disastrous-toll-criminalizing-drug-use.

https://www.kcet.org/shows/artbound/arts-in-corrections-program-returns-to-california-prisons

https://onbeing.org/programs/

richard-davidson-a-neuroscientist-on-love-and-learning-feb2019/#tran-
script

   https://www.afsc.org/resource/solitary-confinement-facts.

   https://www.stateofthereunion.com (January 8, 2014).

   Melanie DeMore: https://www.youtube.com/watch?v=9w22S8foSbk

   Heartbeat Opera: https://www.heartbeatopera.org/fidelio/

   https://www.thoughtco.com/where-felons-can-and-cannot-
vote-3367689

   https://www.hrw.org/report/2012/01/27/old-behind-bars/
aging-prison-population-united-states

SELECTED SONGS

Lindquist, Kristopher, *Beauty Before Me* (Chants for Meditation and Celebration, 2000).

The Temptations, *Just My Imagination*. Motown, 1971.

Redding, Otis and Cropper, Steve, *Sittin' on the Dock of the Bay.* Volt, 1968.

Larionov, Ivan, *Kalinka*. 1860.

Van Morrison, *Astral Weeks*. Warner Bros. Records, 1968.

Cole, Laurence, *Let Us See the Beauty* (based on a poem by oriah mountain dreamer, oriahmountaindreamer.com).

Geisel, Theodore, and Hague, Albert, *You're a Mean One, Mr. Grinch.* "How the Grinch Stole Christmas", 1966.

Traditional, *Elijah Rock.*

Traditional, *Oh Shenandoah.*

Traditional, *Sometimes I Feel Like a Motherless Child/Deep River*

Alexander, Cecil Frances, *All things Bright and Beautiful.* 1848.

Jackson-Miller, Jill, and Miller, Sy, *Let there be Peace on Earth.* 1955.

Ballard, Glen, and Garret, Siedah, *Man in the Mirror.* Epic, 1987.

Idle, Eric, *Always Look on the Bright Side of Life.* Virgin, 1979.

Bricusse, Leslie, *Happiness.* (from Scrooge, 2002).

Williams, Lucinda, *Sweet Old World.* Chameleon, 1992.

McAfee, Barbara, *Surrounding You.* World of Wonders, 2013.

DeMore, Melanie, *Lead with Love,* 2017.

Keen, Marta, *Homeward Bound.* Alfred Publishing Co, Inc.

Reagon, Bernice Johnson, *We are the Ones We Been Waiting For*

McAfee, Barbara, *I Wish that I Could Show You.* World of Wonders, 2013.

Lowry, Robert Wadsworth, *How Can I Keep from Singing?* 1868.

The Impressions, *People Get Ready.* ABC-Paramount, 1865.

Cooke, Sam, *A Change is Gonna Come.* RCA Victor, 1964.

ABOUT THE AUTHOR

Andy Douglas is a writer and musician living in Iowa City, Iowa. He holds an MFA in Nonfiction Writing from the University of Iowa, where he was the recipient of the Marcus Bach Fellowship for Writing about Religion and Culture. His first book, "The Curve of the World: Into the Spiritual Heart of Yoga" was published in 2013 (Bottom Dog Press). He's active in the Community Sing movement, writes about social justice issues, does some spiritual direction work and leads a kiirtan and meditation circle.